Birds of South Carolina

Todd Telander

FALCONGUIDES®

GUILFORD, CONNECTICUT
HELENA, MONTANA

AN IMPRINT OF GLOBE PEQUOT PRESS

To my wife, Kirsten, my children, Miles and Oliver, and my parents,
all of whom have supported and encouraged me through the years.
Special thanks to Mike Denny for his expert critique of the illustrations.

To buy books in quantity for corporate use
or incentives, call **(800) 962-0973**
or e-mail **premiums@GlobePequot.com**.

FSC
www.fsc.org

MIX

Paper from
responsible sources

FSC® C005010

FALCONGUIDES®

Copyright © 2013 Morris Book Publishing, LLC
Illustrations © 2013 Todd Telander

FalconGuides is an imprint of Globe Pequot Press.
Falcon Field Guides is a trademark and Falcon, FalconGuides, and Outfit
Your Mind are registered trademarks of Morris Book Publishing, LLC.

Illustrations: Todd Telander
Text design: Sheryl P. Kober
Project editors: Heather Santiago, Jennifer Kroll
Layout: Sue Murray

Library of Congress Cataloging-in-Publication Data is available on file.

ISBN 978-0-7627-7892-8

Printed in the United States of America

10 9 8 7 6 5 4 3 2 1

Contents

Introduction. v
Notes about the Species Accounts vi
Bird Topography and Terms viii

Nonpasserines

Geese, Ducks, Mergansers (Family Anatidae) 1
Quail (Family Odontophoridae) 9
Turkeys (Family Phasianidae) 10
Loons (Family Gaviidae) 10
Grebes (Family Podicipedidae) 11
Gannets (Family Sulidae) 12
Storks (Family Ciconiidae) 13
Cormorants (Family Phalacrocoracidae). 13
Anhinga (Family Anhingadae) 14
Pelicans (Family Pelecanidae) 14
Herons, Egrets (Family Ardeidae) 15
Ibises, Spoonbills (Family Threskiornithidae). 20
New World Vultures (Family Cathartidae). 21
Osprey (Family Pandionidae) 22
Kites, Hawks, Eagles (Family Accipitridae). 22
Falcons (Family Falconidae) 26
Rails, Coots (Family Rallidae). 27
Plovers (Family Charadriidae) 30
Oystercatchers (Family Haematopodidae) 32
Avocets, Stilts (Family Recurvirostridae). 32
Sandpipers, Phalaropes (Family Scolopacidae) 33
Gulls, Terns (Family Laridae) 38
Pigeons, Doves (Family Columbidae) 43
Cuckoos (Family Cuculidae) 45
Barn Owls (Family Tytonidae) 45
Typical Owls (Family Strigidae) 46

Nightjars, Nighthawks (Family Caprimulgidae) 47
Swifts (Family Apodidae) 48
Hummingbirds (Family Trochilidae) 49
Kingfishers (Family Alcedinidae) 49
Woodpeckers (Family Picidae). 50

Passerines

Tyrant Flycatchers (Family Tyrannidae) 53
Shrikes (Family Laniidae) 56
Vireos (Family Vireonidae) 56
Jays, Crows (Family Corvidae) 58
Swallows (Family Hirundinidae). 59
Chickadees, Titmice (Family Paridae). 61
Nuthatches (Family Sittidae). 62
Creepers (Family Certhiidae). 64
Wrens (Family Troglodytidae) 64
Gnatcatchers (Family Polioptilidae) 66
Kinglets (Family Regulidae) 67
Thrushes (Family Turdidae). 68
Mockingbirds, Catbirds, Thrashers (Family Mimidae) 70
Starlings (Family Sturnidae) 71
Waxwings (Family Bombycillidae) 72
Wood-Warblers (Family Parulidae) 72
Sparrows (Family Emberizidae) 79
Cardinals, Tanagers, Grosbeaks, Buntings
    (Family Cardinalidae). 83
Blackbirds, Grackles, Orioles (Family Icteridae) 85
Finches (Family Fringillidae) 89
Old World Sparrows (Family Passeridae) 90

Index 91
About the Author/Illustrator 96

Introduction

South Carolina gently rises from the Atlantic Ocean at its eastern border to the Blue Ridge Mountains at its northwestern corner. The subtropical low country of the east is dominated by a great coastal plain with an undulating coastline of bays, estuaries, and beaches. Here you will find all manner of shorebirds, gulls, terns, and waterfowl, including tropical species such as the Anhinga and the Wood Stork. The inner part of this plain is marked by the sandhill region—relic of an ancient seafloor—and terminates at the "fall line" with the clay soils of the hilly piedmont region. Farther westward the land slopes into mountains that are home to an array of forest birds and breeding warblers.

This geographic diversity, with its accompanying array of climatic and vegetative zones, provides for an incredible number and variety of bird species. South Carolina supports habitat for resident breeders and seasonal visitors, as well as those birds passing through on migration to and from South America and Canada. Although South Carolina is home to or visited by more than 400 species of birds, this guide describes 177 of the most common birds you are likely to encounter and will give you a good start to understanding the birdlife here.

Notes about the Species Accounts

Order
The order of species listed in this guide is based on the latest version of the *Checklist of North American Birds,* published by the American Ornithologists' Union. In an effort to remain current, I have used the most recent arrangement, so the arrangement of some groups, especially within the nonpasserines, may be slightly different than that of older field guides.

Names
For each entry I have included the common name as well as the scientific name. Since common names tend to vary regionally or there may be more than one common name for each species, the universally accepted scientific name of genus and species (such as *Hylocichla mustelina,* for the Wood Thrush) is more reliable to be certain of identification. Also, you can often learn interesting facts about a bird by the English translation of its Latin name. For instance, *hylocichla* refers to "forest," the Wood Thrush's favored habitat, and *mustelina* refers to the weasel-like color of its plumage.

Families
Birds are grouped into families based on similar traits, behaviors, and genetics. When trying to identify an unfamiliar bird, it is often helpful to first place it into a family, which will limit your search to a smaller group. For example, if you see a long-legged, long-billed bird lurking in the shallows, you can begin your search in the family group of Ardeidae (Herons, Egrets) and narrow your search from there.

Size
The size listed for each bird is the average length from the tip of its bill to the end of its tail, if the bird was laid out flat. Sometimes females and males vary in size, and this is mentioned in

the text. Size can be misleading if you are looking at a small bird that happens to have a very long tail or bill. It may be more effective to use the bird's relative size or judge the size difference between two or more species.

Season
The season provided in the accounts is when the greatest number of individuals occur in South Carolina. Some species are year-round residents that breed here. Others may spend only summers or winters in the state, and some may be transient, only stopping during the spring or fall migration. Even if only part of the year is indicated for a species, be aware that individuals may arrive earlier or remain for longer than that time frame. Plumage also changes with the season for many birds, and this is indicated in the text and illustrations.

Habitat
A bird's habitat is one of the first clues to its identification. Note the environment where you see a bird and compare it with the description listed. This can be especially helpful when identifying a bird that shares traits with related species. For example, Cattle Egrets and Snowy Egrets are similar, but Cattle Egrets are found in drier fields and pastures, while Snowy Egrets prefer swamps and open water.

Illustrations
Illustrations show the adult bird in the plumage most likely to be encountered during the season(s) it is in South Carolina. If it is likely that you will see more than one type of plumage during this time, the alternate plumage is shown as well. For birds that are sexually dimorphic (females and males look different), I have usually included illustrations of both sexes. Other plumages, such as juveniles and alternate morphs, are described in the text.

Bird Topography and Terms

Bird topography describes the outer surface of a bird and how its various anatomical structures fit together. Below is a diagram outlining the terms most commonly used to describe the feathers and bare parts of a bird.

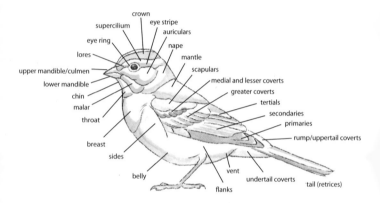

NONPASSERINES

Canada Goose, *Branta canadensis*
Family Anatidae (Geese, Ducks, Mergansers)
Size: 27–32", depending on race
Season: Year-round
Habitat: Marshes, grasslands, public parks, golf courses

The Canada Goose is the state's most common goose and is found in suburban settings. It is vegetarian, foraging on land for grass, seeds, and grain or in the water by upending like the dabbling ducks. It has a heavy body with short, thick legs and a long neck. Plumage is barred gray-brown overall with a white rear, short black tail, black neck, and a white patch running under the neck to behind the eye. During the bird's powerful flight, the white rump makes a semicircular patch between the tail and back. The voice is a loud honk. In flight Canada Geese form the classic V formation. (Illustration shows an adult.)

Wood Duck, *Aix sponsa*
Family Anatidae
(Geese, Ducks, Mergansers)
Size: 18"
Season: Year-round
Habitat: Wooded ponds and swamps

The regal Wood Duck is among the dabbling ducks, or those that tip headfirst into shallow water to pluck aquatic plants and animals from the bottom. The male is long-tailed and small-billed, with a dark back, light buff-colored flanks, and sharp black-and-white head patterning. It also sports a bushy head crest that droops behind the nape. The female is gray-brown, with spotting along the undersides and a conspicuous white, teardrop-shaped eye patch. Both sexes swim with their heads angled downward as if in a nod, and they have sharp claws, which they use to cling to branches and snags. (Illustration shows a breeding male, below, and a female, above.)

Gadwall, *Anas strepera*
Family Anatidae
(Geese, Ducks, Mergansers)
Size: 20.5"
Season: Winter
Habitat: Shallow lakes, marshes

The Gadwall is a buoyant, plain-colored dabbling duck with a steep forehead and a somewhat angular head. The breeding male is grayish overall, with very fine variegation and barring. The rump and undertail coverts are black, the scapulars are light orange-brown, the tertials are gray, and the head is lighter below the eye and darker above. Females and nonbreeding males are mottled brown with few distinguishing markings. In flight there is a distinctive white speculum that is more prominent in males. Gadwalls dabble or dive for a variety of aquatic plants and invertebrates and often gather in large flocks away from the shore. (Illustration shows a breeding male, below, and female, above.)

American Widgeon, *Anas americana*
Family Anatidae (Geese, Ducks, Mergansers)
Size: 19"
Season: Winter
Habitat: Shallow ponds, fields

The American Widgeon is also known as the Baldpate, in reference to its white crown. A wary and easily alarmed duck, it feeds from the water's surface, often gleaning prey stirred up by the efforts of diving ducks. The underside is a light cinnamon color with white undertail coverts, and the back is light brown. The male has a white crown and forehead, with a very slight crest when seen in profile. A glossy dark green patch extends from the eye to the back of the neck. A white wing covert patch can usually be seen on the folded wing but is more obvious in flight. The head of the female is unmarked and brownish. (Illustration shows a breeding male, below, and a female, above.)

Mallard, *Anas platyrhynchos*
Family Anatidae
(Geese, Ducks, Mergansers)
Size: 23"
Season: Year-round
Habitat: Parks, urban areas, virtually any water environment

The ubiquitous Mallard is the most abundant duck in the Northern Hemisphere. It is a classic dabbling duck, plunging its head into the water with its tail up, searching for aquatic plants, animals, and snails. It will also eat worms, seeds, insects, and even mice. Noisy and quacking, it is a heavy but strong flier. The male has a dark head with green or blue iridescence, a white neck ring, and a large yellow bill. The underparts are pale with a chestnut-brown breast. The female is plain brownish with buff-colored, scalloped markings. She also has a dark eye line and orangey bill with a dark center. The speculum is blue on both sexes, and the tail coverts often curl upward. Mallards form huge floating flocks called "rafts." To achieve flight, a Mallard lifts straight into the air without running. (Illustration shows a breeding male, below, and a female, above.)

Northern Shoveler,

Anas clypeata
Family Anatidae
(Geese, Ducks, Mergansers)
Size: 19"
Season: Winter
Habitat: Shallow marshes, lakes, and bays

Also known as the Spoonbill Duck, the Northern Shoveler skims the surface of the water with its neck extended, scooping up aquatic animals and plants with its long, spatula-like bill. It also sucks up ooze from the muddy bottoms of its habitats and strains it through bristles at the edge of its bill, retaining worms, leeches, and snails. This medium-size duck seems top-heavy due to its large bill. Plumage in the male is white on the underside, with a large, chestnut-colored side patch, a dark green head, and a gray bill. The female is pale brownish overall with an orangey bill. (Illustration shows a breeding male, below, and a female, above.)

Northern Pintail, *Anas acuta*

Family Anatidae
(Geese, Ducks, Mergansers)
Size: 21"
Season: Winter
Habitat: Marshes, shallow lakes

Among the most abundant ducks in North America, the Northern Pintail is an elegant, slender, dabbling duck with a long neck, small head, and narrow wings. In breeding plumage the male has long, pointed central tail feathers. It is gray along its back and sides, with a brown head and a white breast. A white stripe extends from the breast along the back of the neck. The female is mottled brown and tan overall, with a light brown head. To feed, the Northern Pintail bobs its head into the water to capture aquatic invertebrates and plants from the muddy bottom. It rises directly out of the water to take flight. (Illustration shows a breeding male, below, and a female, above.)

GEESE, DUCKS, MERGANSERS

4

Green-winged Teal, *Anas crecca*
Family Anatidae (Geese, Ducks, Mergansers)
Size: 14"
Season: Winter
Habitat: Marshes, ponds

The Green-winged Teal is a cute, very small, active duck with a small, thin bill. The breeding male is silvery-gray with a dotted, tawny breast patch, a pale yellow hip patch, and a distinct, vertical white bar on its side. The head is rusty brown with an iridescent green patch around and behind the eye. Females and nonbreeding males are mottled brown with a dark eye line and a white belly. Green-winged Teals dabble in the shallows for plant material and small invertebrates. They are quick and agile in flight and sport a bright green speculum. They form very large winter flocks. (Illustration shows a breeding male, below, and a female, above.)

Ring-necked Duck,
Aytha collaris
Family Anatidae
(Geese, Ducks, Mergansers)
Size: 17"
Season: Winter
Habitat: Coastal marshes

The Ring-necked Duck, also known as the Ring-billed Duck, is classified as a diving duck, typically swimming underwater to find plants and animal prey, although it may also behave like a dabbling duck and bob for food at the surface. This small, gregarious duck looks tall with a postlike head and neck and a peaked crown. The breeding male is stunning, with its contrasting light and dark plumage and a dark, metallic brown-purple head. The base of its bill is edged with white feathers, and the bill itself is gray with a white ring and black tip. The ring around the neck, for which it is named, is actually a very inconspicuous brownish band at the bottom of the neck in the male bird The female is more brownish overall, with white eye rings. (Illustration shows a breeding male, below, and a female, above.)

Lesser Scaup, *Aythya affinis*
Family Anatidae
(Geese, Ducks, Mergansers)
Size: 17"
Season: Winter
Habitat: Marshes, shallow lakes, coastal bays

The Lesser Scaup is a small, short-bodied duck with a tall head profile and a relatively thin bill. The breeding male is distinctly two-toned, with white sides, a pale, variegated gray back, and a black rear end and front. The head has a dark, metallic violet or greenish cast in good light, and the bill has a small black dot at the nail. The nonbreeding male is paler, with brown on its sides. Females are gray-brown with a dark brown head and a white patch at the base of the bill. This diving duck forages for aquatic plants and insects. It is very similar to the Greater Scaup but is smaller and has a more peaked head. (Illustration shows a breeding male, below, and a female, above.)

Surf Scoter, *Melanitta perspicillata*
Family Anatidae
(Geese, Ducks, Mergansers)
Size: 20"
Season: Winter
Habitat: Coastal waters

The Surf Scoter is a stocky, large-headed coastal diving duck with short, pointed wings and a colorful, thick-based bill. The male is black overall, with white patches at the back of the neck and on the forehead. His eyes are light and the bill is orange, with white and a round black spot on the sides. The female is brown overall, with a black cap, and a grayish bill. She has faint white patches along the base of the bill and cheeks and sometimes on the nape. Surf Scoters dive for shellfish and crustaceans, propelled by their short wings. Because of their markings, they are sometimes called "skunk-headed ducks." (Illustration shows a breeding male, below, and a breeding female, above.)

GEESE, DUCKS, MERGANSERS

Bufflehead, *Bucephala albeola*
Family Anatidae
(Geese, Ducks, Mergansers)
Size: 14"
Season: Winter
Habitat: Inland lakes or
sheltered coastal bays

The Bufflehead is a diminutive diving duck—indeed, the smallest duck in North America. Also known as the Bumblebee Duck, it forms small flocks that forage in open water for aquatic plants and invertebrates. The duck's puffy, rounded head seems large for its body and small, gray-blue bill. The breeding male is striking, with a large white patch on the back half of its head that contrasts with the black front of its head and its black back. The male's underside is white. The female is paler overall, with a dark gray-brown head and an airfoil-shaped white patch behind the eyes. Flight is low to the water with rapid wing beats. (Illustration shows a breeding male, below, and a female, above.)

Common Goldeneye,
Bucephala clangula
Family Anatidae
(Geese, Ducks, Mergansers)
Size: 18.5"
Season: Winter
Habitat: Lakes, rivers

The Common Goldeneye is a compact, large-headed diving duck with a tall, rounded head, and a stubby bill. The breeding male is plumed in stark black and white: It has a white body, with thin black streaks above, and a greenish black head and rear end. It has bright yellow eyes and a circular white patch between the eye and the bill. The female is gray overall, with a brown head and a yellow-tipped bill. This duck is sometimes called the "Whistler" because of the whistling sound made by its wings in flight. It forms small flocks in winter. (Illustration shows a breeding male, below, and a female, above.)

Red-breasted Merganser,

Mergus serrator
Family Anatidae
(Geese, Ducks, Mergansers)
Size: 23"
Season: Winter
Habitat: Coastal wetlands, bays

Mergansers are known as the Fishing Ducks or Sawtooths. They dive and chase fish of considerable size underwater and secure their catches with long, thin bills that are serrated along the edges. Both male and female Red-breasted Mergansers sport a fine, long, two-part crest. The male has a white band around its neck, a dark head, red bill, and gray flanks. The female is grayish overall, with a reddish brown head. The nonbreeding male closely resembles the female. Flight is low and quick on pointed wings. (Illustration shows a breeding male, below, and a female, above.)

Hooded Merganser,

Lophodytes cucullatus
Family Anatidae
(Geese, Ducks, Mergansers)
Size: 18"
Season: Winter
Habitat: Sheltered coastal waters

The mergansers are known as the Fishing Ducks or Sawtooths. The Hooded Merganser is North America's smallest merganser and has a small, thin bill, a long tail, and a dramatic crest. Males are black above and orange-brown below, with a white breast divided by vertical black stripes. The long tertials are striped with white. The head is rounded, with a clean, white patch behind the bright yellow eyes; the crest can be held low or raised tall. Females are grayish brown, lighter below, and have a rusty brown crest that fans out to the back, although it is not nearly as tall as that of the males. Nonbreeding males are similar to females. Hooded Mergansers dive underwater for fish, amphibians, and invertebrates. (Illustration shows a breeding male, below, and a female, above.)

Ruddy Duck, *Oxyura jamaicencis*
Family Anatidae
(Geese, Ducks, Mergansers)
Size: 15"
Season: Winter
Habitat: Open water, fresh- or
saltwater wetlands

The Ruddy Duck is a "stiff-tailed duck," part of a group known for rigid tail feathers that are often cocked up in display. It dives deep for its food, which consists of aquatic vegetation, and flies low over the water with quick wing beats. It is a relatively small duck with a big head and a flat, broad body. The breeding male is rich sienna brown overall, with white cheeks, a black cap and nape, and a bright blue bill. The female is a drab, grayish brown, with a conspicuous dark stripe across the cheek. Nonbreeding males become gray. The Ruddy Duck can sink low into the water, grebe-like, and will often dive to escape danger. (Illustration shows a breeding male, below, and a female, above.)

Northern Bobwhite,
Colinus virginianus
Family Odontophoridae (Quail)
Size: 10"
Season: Year-round
Habitat: Brushy fields and open
woodlands

The Bobwhite, like other quail, is a secretive, ground-dwelling bird that usually takes flight only if alarmed. It travels in coveys of ten or more while scavenging for seeds, berries, and insects. It is plump with a very short, gray tail and a short, thick, curved bill. Plumage in males is heavily streaked rufous, gray, and black, with a plain rufous breast below a mottled black upper neck. It has a white superciliary stripe and throat. The female is paler, with a greater extent of rufous coloring and a buff-colored eye line and throat. The call sounds somewhat like its name: *Bob-White*. (Illustration shows an adult male.)

Wild Turkey,
Meleagris gallopavo
Family Phasianidae (Turkeys)
Size: 36–48"; male larger than female
Season: Year-round
Habitat: Open hardwood forests

The Wild Turkey is a very large, dark, ground-dwelling bird (but slimmer than the domestic variety). The head and neck appear small for the body size, and the legs are thick and stout. The heavily barred plumage is quite iridescent in strong light. Head and neck are covered with bluish, warty, crinkled bare skin that droops under the chin in a red wattle. Often foraging in flocks, Wild Turkeys roam the ground for seeds, grubs, and insects, and then roost at night in trees. Males emit the familiar *Gobble,* while females are less vocal, making a soft clucking sound. In display the male hunches up with its tail up and spread like a giant fan. (Illustration shows an adult male.)

Red-Throated Loon,
Gavia stellata
Family Gaviidae (Loons)
Size: 25"
Season: Winter
Habitat: Coastal bays, estuaries

The Red-throated Loon is a small loon with a thin, pointed bill that it habitually holds at an upward-tilted angle. The breeding adult is dark, with white mottling above and white below. The head is pale gray, with a rust-colored throat patch and black-and-white striping down the nape. The bill is black. Nonbreeding adults lack the throat patch, the head is dark above the eyes and white across the face and foreneck, and the bill is pale gray. Quite clumsy on land, they dive deep underwater in search of fish, propelled by their strong, webbed feet. In flight Red-throated Loons hold their heads outstretched below the line of the body. (Illustration shows a breeding adult, below, and a nonbreeding adult, above.)

Common Loon, *Gavia immer*
Family Gaviidae (Loons)
Size: 30"
Season: Winter
Habitat: Coastal waters

Riding low in the water outside the surf zone, this heavy waterbird periodically dives for fish, propelled by its strong, webbed feet. Designed for a life in the water, it has legs set far back on its body, which makes walking on land a clumsy affair and takeoff into the air labored. Unlike the flashy, black-and-white-spotted plumage it sports during summer in northern lakes, we usually see this bird in its drab gray-and-white coloration. Its call, a haunting yodel, is rarely heard while the Common Loon winters in South Carolina. It can be distinguished from other loons by the horizontal posture of its large bill (not held upwards). It's fairly common in winter, scattered singly or in pairs along the coast. (Illustration shows a nonbreeding adult.)

Horned Grebe, *Podiceps auritus*
Family Podicipedidae (Grebes)
Size: 14"
Season: Winter
Habitat: Coastal bays, inland marshes and lakes

The Horned Grebe is a sleek, compact, relatively heavy waterbird with a short, straight bill. Like other grebes, it uses its heavily lobed feet, placed far to the back of its body, to swim rapidly underwater after fish. Breeding adults are slate gray on the back, with rufous flanks and neck and a white belly. A patch of golden-yellow feathers plume back behind the eye, creating the "horn," and is bordered by a black crown and upper neck. Nonbreeding adults are grayish above and streaked gray on the flanks, with a white foreneck. Their heads are dark gray above the eye, with white across the face. All plumages show a pale tip to the bill. In flight Horned Grebes hold their upper bodies and head at an upward angle. (Illustration shows a breeding adult, below, and a nonbreeding adult, above.)

Pied-billed Grebe,
Podilymbus podiceps
Family Podicipedidae (Grebes)
Size: 13"
Season: Year-round
Habitat: Freshwater ponds and lakes

The Pied-billed Grebe is a secretive, small grebe that lurks in sheltered waters diving for small fish, leeches, snails, and crawfish. When alarmed, or to avoid predatory snakes and hawks, it sinks below the surface until only the head is above water. It is brownish overall, slightly darker above, with a tiny tail and short wings. Breeding adults have a conspicuous dark ring around the middle of the bill. The ring is missing in winter plumage. The grebe nests on a floating mat of vegetation. (Illustration shows a breeding adult.)

Northern Gannet,
Morus bassanus
Family Sulidae (Gannets)
Size: 36"
Season: Winter
Habitat: Open ocean close to shore

The name Gannet derives from "gander" and alludes to this seabird's gooselike shape. Often forming very large groups, the Northern Gannet alternates rapid wing beats with soaring flight. To feed it forms its body into a sleek arrow shape and dramatically plunges headfirst into the ocean, completely submerging to catch fish. The gannet's body is sleek and white, with black flight feathers. The upper part of the head is pale yellow; the bluish bill is thick and pointed. The seemingly small eyes are enveloped in a thin black ring and lores. Juveniles are dark and spotted with white. (Illustration shows an adult.)

Wood Stork,
Mycteria americana
Family Ciconiidae (Storks)
Size: 40"
Season: Summer
Habitat: Salt- or freshwater open marshes

The Wood Stork is a large, somewhat unattractive bird with a white body, black flight feathers, and a featherless neck and head covered in blackish, scaly skin. The bill is long, decurved, and blunt at its tip. The stork forms flocks and feeds by probing its bill into the mud, stirring up prey such as fish and snakes. It flies with its neck outstretched in loose, unorganized groups. At rest it will stand motionless for an hour or more in a distinctive upright posture, with its bill tucked down and against the body. Wood Storks roost in mangrove or cypress trees. The voice is a croaking sound or a chattering created by snapping the upper and lower mandibles together. (Illustration shows an adult.)

Double-crested Cormorant,
Phalacrocorax auritus
Family Phalacrocoracidae (Cormorants)
Size: 32"
Season: Year-round
Habitat: Open fresh- or salt water

Named for the two long, white plumes that emerge from behind the eyes during breeding season, the Double-crested Cormorant is an expert swimmer that dives underwater to chase down fish. Because its plumage lacks the normal oils to repel water, it will stand with wings outstretched to dry itself. These cormorants are solid black with a pale, glossy cast on the back and wings. The eyes are bright green, the bill is thin and hooked, and the throat patch and lores are orange-yellow. (Illustration shows a breeding adult.)

Anhinga,
Anhinga anhinga
Family Anhingadae (Anhinga)
Size: 34"
Season: Summer
Habitat: Freshwater or brackish ponds and swamps

With a cormorant-like body and snakelike neck, the Anhinga swims underwater to spear fish with its sharp, daggerlike bill. They can be seen with only the head above water or soaring high above the marshes and often stand with wings outstretched to dry. The Anhinga's body is black with finely patterned white streaks; its tail is long, barred with white, and tipped with brown. Females have a pale brown neck and head; in males those parts are all black. Males in breeding plumage develop an upturned crest. (Illustration shows an adult female.)

Brown Pelican,
Pelecanus occidentalis
Family Pelecanidae (Pelicans)
Size: 50"
Season: Year-round
Habitat: Coastal waters

The majestic Brown Pelican enlivens the coastal waters with its spectacular feeding process—plunge-diving headfirst from some height for fish. In flight they often cruise in formation inches from incoming swells, gaining lift and rarely needing to flap their wings. The plumage is a bleached gray-brown overall with a white head and neck; the bill is massive. In breeding plumage the head is pale yellow with a brown-red nape patch and a black strip down the back of the neck. Quite gregarious, Brown Pelicans may nest in mangrove trees or in slight depressions in the sand or rocks. (Illustration shows a breeding adult.)

American Bittern, *Botaurus lentiginosus*
Family Ardeidae (Herons, Egrets)
Size: 27"
Season: Winter
Habitat: Marshy areas with
dense vegetation

The American Bittern is a fairly large, secretive heron with a small head, a long, straight bill, and a thick body. It has a habit of standing still with its neck and bill pointed straight up to imitate the surrounding reeds. Its plumage is very cryptic: Above, it is variegated brown and tan; below, it is pale brown or whitish with thick, rust-colored streaking that extends up the neck. The bill is yellow-green and dark on the upper mandible. A dark patch extends from the lower bill to the upper neck. The legs are yellow-green and thick. American Bitterns skulk slowly through reeds and grasses to catch frogs, insects, and invertebrates. (Illustration shows an adult.)

Least Bittern, *Ixobrychus exilis*
Family Ardeidae (Herons, Egrets)
Size: 13"
Season: Summer
Habitat: Fresh or brackish marshes

North America's smallest heron, the secretive Least Bittern is more often heard than seen. It creeps and clambers through densely vegetated marshes searching for frogs, invertebrates, and other aquatic creatures, emitting a soft cooing call, or a *Kaw* when disturbed. When alarmed it will stand motionless with its head straight up to imitate surrounding reeds. Least Bitterns are rarely seen in flight. The back is a dark blue-gray; the midwing and body are buff-brown with white streaking. The crown is dark gray, and the bill is yellow and pointed. The legs and feet are yellow with long, thin toes for grasping clumps of vegetation. The female is paler along the back and crown. (Illustration shows an adult male.)

Great Blue Heron,
Ardea herodias
Family Ardeidae (Herons, Egrets)
Size: 46"
Season: Year-round
Habitat: Most aquatic areas, lakes, creeks, marshes

The Great Blue Heron is the largest heron in North America. Walking slowly through shallow water or fields, it stalks fish, crabs, and small vertebrates, catching them with its massive bill. With long legs and a long neck, the heron is blue-gray overall, with a white face and a heavy, yellow-orange bill. The crown is black, supporting plumes of medium length. The front of the neck is white, with distinct black chevrons fading into breast plumes. In flight the neck is tucked back; wing beats are regular and labored. (Illustration shows an adult.)

Great Egret,
Ardea alba
Family Ardeidae (Herons, Egrets)
Size: 38"
Season: Year-round
Habitat: Fresh- or saltwater marshes

One of North America's most widespread herons, the Great Egret is all white with a long, thin, yellow bill and long black legs. During breeding season it develops long, lacy plumes across its back. Stalking slowly through salt- and freshwater marshes, Great Egrets pursue fish, frogs, and other aquatic animals. (Illustration shows a breeding adult.)

Snowy Egret,
Egretta thula
Family Ardeidae (Herons, Egrets)
Size: 24"
Season: Year-round
Habitat: Open water, marshes, swamps

The Snowy Egret is all white, with lacy plumes across the back in breeding season. The bill is slim and black, and the legs are black with bright yellow feet. Juveniles have greenish legs with a yellow stripe along the front. The egret forages for fish and frogs along shorelines by moving quickly, shuffling to stir up prey, and stabbing the prey with its bill. Sometimes it may run to pursue its quarry. You can remember the name of this bird by keeping in mind that it wears yellow "boots" because it is cold, or "snowy." (Illustration shows a breeding adult.)

Little Blue Heron,
Egretta caerulea
Family Ardeidae (Herons, Egrets)
Size: 25"
Season: Year-round
Habitat: Freshwater or coastal swamps

The Little Blue Heron is a medium-size heron that skulks along shorelines with vegetative cover, often using its wings to cast a shadow over the water to help it see and attract fish. It is slate blue overall with a purple cast on the neck. The bill is pale gray with a dark tip; the legs are greenish. Juveniles are all white, with small dark tips on the primaries, and can be confused with other white herons. (Illustration shows an adult.)

Tricolored Heron,
Egretta tricolor
Family Ardeidae (Herons, Egrets)
Size: 26"
Season: Year-round
Habitat: Salt marshes,
swamps

The Tricolored Heron is a thin, bluish gray heron with a white belly and orangey neck stripe and lower back. In nonbreeding plumage it has yellow lores and an orangey bill, but in breeding season this area of the lores and bill are blue and the bill has a dark tip. It also develops plumes behind the ears and across the lower back. To feed, it actively pursues prey or stands motionless, waiting to stab a fish or frog with its thin, spearlike bill. (Illustration shows a breeding adult.)

Cattle Egret, *Bubulcus ibis*
Family Ardeidae (Herons, Egrets)
Size: 20"
Season: Summer
Habitat: Upland fields, often near
cattle in grazing land

The Cattle Egret is a widespread species originally from Africa and now quite common in the southeastern United States. Unlike most herons, it is not normally found in aquatic environments. It forms groups around cattle, often perching atop them, and feeds on insects aroused by the movement of their hooves. It is stocky, all white, and has a comparatively short yellow bill and short black legs. In breeding plumage the legs and bill turn a bright orange, and a peachy, pale yellow forms on the crown, breast, and back. (Illustration shows a nonbreeding adult.)

Green Heron, *Butorides virescens*
Family Ardeidae (Herons, Egrets)
Size: 18"
Season: Summer
Habitat: Ponds, creeks, coastal wetlands (fresh- or saltwater)

The Green Heron is a compact, crow-size bird that perches on low branches over the water, crouching forward to search for fish, snails, and insects. It is known to toss a bug into the water to attract fish. The Green Heron is really not so green but a dull grayish blue with a burgundy/chestnut-colored neck and black crown. The bill is dark, and the legs are bright yellow-orange. When disturbed, the heron will raise its crest feathers, stand erect, and twitch its tail. The species is fairly secretive and solitary. (Illustration shows an adult.)

Black-crowned Night-Heron,
Nycticorax nycticorax
Family Ardeidae (Herons, Egrets)
Size: 25"
Season: Year-round
Habitat: Marshes, swamps with wooded banks

The nocturnal Black-crowned Night-Heron is a stocky, thick-necked heron with a comparatively large head and sharp, heavy, thick bill. It has pale gray wings, white underparts, and a black crown, back, and bill. The eyes are piercing red, and the legs are yellow. It has long, white plumes on the rear of its head. During the day the herons roost in groups, but at night they forage alone, waiting motionless for prey such as fish or crabs. They may even raid the nests of other birds for their young. The heron's voice is composed of low-pitched barks and croaks. (Illustration shows an adult.)

Yellow-crowned Night-Heron,
Nyctanassa violacea
Family Ardeidae (Herons, Egrets)
Size: 24"
Season: Summer; year-round along the coastal plain
Habitat: Marshes, ponds, coastal shrubs

Shaped somewhat like the Black-crowned Night-Heron, the Yellow-crowned Night-Heron is blue-gray overall, with a black face, white cheek patch, and slim, pale crown that is not really yellow but whitish or pale buff, with thin, long plumes behind the crest. The eyes are large and red, and the legs are yellow. Juveniles are drab brown-gray, mottled with light streaks. The herons are nocturnal but will occasionally feed during the day for crustaceans and other aquatic animals, roosting in groups at night. (Illustration shows an adult.)

White Ibis, *Eudocimus albus*
Family Threskiornithidae (Ibises, Spoonbills)
Size: 25"
Season: Year-round
Habitat: Salt marshes, swamps, fields

The White Ibis forages in groups, probing mud and shallow water for small aquatic animals and invertebrates. It is all white except for the black tips of the primaries, which are rarely visible unless the wings are outstretched. The long, downward-curved bill is red with a darker tip, meeting the face in unfeathered, reddish pink facial skin to the eye. The legs are red. Juveniles are dark brown above, with a dark, streaky neck. Ibises fly with necks outstretched, unlike herons, which fly with the neck folded back. (Illustration shows an adult.)

Black Vulture,

Coragyps atratus
Family Cathartidae
(New World Vultures)
Size: 25"
Season: Year-round
Habitat: Open, dry country

Like the Turkey Vulture, the Black Vulture is adept at soaring. Its wing beats, however, are faster, and while soaring it holds its wings at a flat angle instead of a dihedral. It has a stocky physique, a short, stubby tail, and shorter wings than the Turkey Vulture. The primaries are pale on an otherwise black body, and the head is bald and gray. Black Vultures eat carrion and garbage and are quite aggressive at feeding sites. (Illustration shows an adult.)

Turkey Vulture,

Cathartes aura
Family Cathartidae
(New World Vultures)
Size: 27"
Season: Year-round
Habitat: Open, dry country

The Turkey Vulture is known for its effortless, skilled soaring. It will often soar for hours without flapping, rocking in the breeze on its long, 6-foot wings that form an upright V shape, or dihedral angle. It has a black body and inner wing, with pale flight feathers and pale tail feathers that give it a noticeable two-toned appearance from below. The tail is longish, and the feet extend to no more than halfway past the base of the tail. The head is naked, red, and small, making the bird appear almost headless in flight. The bill is strongly hooked to aid in tearing apart its favored food—carrion. Juveniles have a dark gray head. Turkey Vultures often roost in flocks and form groups around food or at a roadkill site. (Illustration shows an adult.)

Osprey, *Pandion haliaetus*
Family Pandionidae (Osprey)
Size: 23"; female larger than male
Season: Year-round
Habitat: Always near water, salt or fresh

Also known as the Fish Hawk, the Osprey exhibits a dramatic feeding method: It plunges feetfirst into the water to snag fish. Sometimes it completely submerges itself then laboriously flies off with its heavy catch. It is dark brown above, white below, and has a distinct dark eye stripe contiguous with the nape. A mottled "necklace" is sometimes noticeable across the breast (more prominent in females), and juveniles have pale streaking on the back. Ospreys fly with an obvious crook at the wrist, appearing gull-like. The wings are long and narrow, with a dark carpal patch. (Illustration shows an adult male.)

KITES, HAWKS, EAGLES

Swallow-tailed Kite,
Elanoides forficatus
Family Accipitridae
(Kites, Hawks, Eagles)
Size: 23"
Season: Summer
Habitat: Wooded environments, wetlands

The Swallow-tailed Kite is a graceful, skilled flier that feeds on the wing, catching insects midair or snatching reptiles from tree branches. It even drinks by skimming along the water's surface. It resembles a large swallow with its long, deeply forked tail and long, thin wings. The body and head are white, the back, tail, and wings are black. The bill is small and hooked, and the eyes are dark. Swallow-tailed Kites may flock together while feeding or during migration to and from their winter home in South America. (Illustration shows an adult.)

Mississippi Kite, *Ictinia mississippiensis*
Family Accipitridae (Kites, Hawks, Eagles)
Size: 14"
Season: Summer
Habitat: Swamps, woodland edges,
agricultural land

The Mississippi Kite, North America's smallest kite, has a rounded head, a short, hooked bill, and long wings and tail. Its plumage is slate gray across the back, undersides, and upper wing; the head is paler, becoming almost white. The tail and ends of the primaries are black, contrasting with the white secondaries. The lores and feathers surrounding the deep red eyes are black. Sexes are similar, while juveniles show white spotting on the back and rufous spotting on the underside. In flight the kite's wings are held flat and straight, and the outermost primary is noticeably shorter than the others. Mississippi Kites feed in flight, snatching insects from the air or swooping low to attack small terrestrial animals. The voice is a high-pitched, relatively weak whistle in two parts. (Illustration shows an adult.)

Northern Harrier,
Circus cyaneus
Family Accipitridae
(Kites, Hawks, Eagles)
Size: 18"; female larger than male
Season: Winter
Habitat: Open fields and wetlands

Also known as the Marsh Hawk, the Northern Harrier flies low to the ground, methodically surveying its hunting grounds for rodents and other small animals. When it spots prey, aided by its acute hearing, it will drop abruptly to the ground to attack. It is a thin raptor with long tail and long, flame-shaped wings that are broad in the middle. The face has a distinct owl-like facial disk, and there is a conspicuous white patch at the rump. Males are gray above, with a white, streaked breast and black wing tips. Females are brown with a barred breast. Juveniles are similar in plumage to the female but have a pale belly. (Illustration shows a female, below, and a male, above.)

Bald Eagle,
Haliaeetus leucocephalus
Family Accipitridae
(Kites, Hawks, Eagles)
Size: 30–40"; female larger than male
Season: Year-round
Habitat: Seashores, lakes, rivers with tall perches or cliffs

The Bald Eagle is a large raptor that is fairly uncommon even though its range is widespread. It eats fish or scavenges dead animals and may congregate in large numbers where food is abundant. Plumage is dark brown, which contrasts with its white head and tail. Juveniles show white splotching across the wings and breast. The yellow bill is large and powerful, and the talons are large and sharp. In flight the eagle holds its wings fairly flat and straight, resembling a long plank. Bald Eagles make huge nests of sticks high in trees. (Illustration shows an adult.)

Cooper's Hawk,
Accipiter cooperii
Family Accipitridae
(Kites, Hawks, Eagles)
Size: 17"; female larger than male
Season: Year-round
Habitat: Woodlands

The Cooper's Hawk perches stealthily and then, on the wing through thickets, ambushes its prey of smaller birds or mammals. Its plumage is grayish above and light below, barred with pale rufous. Very similar to the Sharp-shinned Hawk, the Cooper's Hawk is larger and has a slightly longer, rounded tail, thinner wings, and a proportionately larger head. Unlike the Sharp-shinned Hawk, Cooper's Hawks may perch and hunt in open country. (Illustration shows an adult.)

Red-shouldered Hawk,
Buteo lineatus
Family Accipitridae
(Kites, Hawks, Eagles)
Size: 17"
Season: Year-round
Habitat: Wooded areas near water

The Red-shouldered Hawk is a solitary, small, accipiter-like buteo that waits patiently on its perch before flying down to attack a variety of small prey animals. It has a long, banded black-and-white tail and spotted dark wings. The head and shoulder are rust-colored, and the breast is heavily barred with rust, becoming paler toward the belly. The legs are long and yellow, the bill is hooked, and in flight there is a pale arc just inside the wing tips. The hawk flies with quick wing beats followed by short glides. The illustration shows an adult.

Broad-winged Hawk,
Buteo lineatus
Family Accipitridae
(Kites, Hawks, Eagles)
Size: 15"
Season: Summer
Habitat: Woodlands, roadsides

North America's smallest buteo, the Broad-winged Hawk summers in eastern North America and migrates in huge flocks to Central and South America in winter. It is dark brown above and white below, with a reddish brown breast that fades to spotting and barring across the belly and flanks. A rare dark morph is dark brown overall. Both morphs have wide black-and-white bars across the tail, less developed in juveniles. In flight there is a dark border to the trailing edge of the otherwise light underwing, and the wings are held flat while soaring. Broad-winged Hawks hunt for small mammals, reptiles, amphibians, or invertebrates, often near a water source. The voice is a piercing, very high-pitched *Pe-Seeee*. (Illustration shows an adult light morph.)

Red-tailed Hawk,

Buteo jamaicensis
Family Accipitridae
(Kites, Hawks, Eagles)
Size: 20″
Season: Year-round
Habitat: Open country, prairies

This widespread species is the most common buteo in the United States. It has broad, rounded wings and a stout hooked bill. Its plumage is highly variable depending on geographic location. In general the underparts are light, with darker streaking that forms a dark band across the belly. The upperparts are dark brown, and the tail is rufous. Light spotting occurs along the scapulars. In flight there is a noticeable dark patch along the inner leading edge of the underwing. Red-tailed Hawks glide down from perches, such as telephone poles or posts in open country, to catch rodents. They also may hover to spot prey. They are usually seen alone or in pairs. The voice is the familiar *Keeer!* (Illustration shows an adult.)

American Kestrel,

Falco sparverius
Family Falconidae (Falcons)
Size: 10″
Season: Year-round
Habitat: Open country, urban areas

North America's most common falcon, the American Kestrel is a tiny, robin-size falcon with long, pointed wings and tail and fast flight. It hovers above fields or dives from its perch in branches or on a wire to capture small animals and insects. The kestrel's upperparts are rufous barred with black, the wings are blue-gray, and the breast is buff-colored or white and streaked with black spots. The head is patterned, with a gray crown and vertical patches of black down the face. The female has rufous wings and a barred tail. Also known as the Sparrow Hawk, the kestrel has a habit of flicking its tail up and down while perched. (Illustration shows an adult male.)

Peregrine Falcon,
Falco peregrinus
Family Falconidae (Falcons)
Size: 17"; female larger than male
Season: Winter
Habitat: Open country, cliffs, urban areas

The Peregrine Falcon is a powerful and agile raptor with long, sharply pointed wings. It is dark slate gray above and pale whitish below, with uniform barring below the breast. Plumage on the head forms a distinctive "helmet," with a white ear patch and chin contrasting with the blackish face and crown. Juveniles are mottled brown overall, with heavy streaking on the underside. Peregrine Falcons attack other birds in flight using spectacular high-speed aerial dives. Once threatened by DDT pollution that caused thinning of their eggshells, the Peregrine Falcon has made a dramatic comeback. (Illustration shows an adult.)

Black Rail,
Laterallus jamaicensis
Family Rallidae (Rails, Coots)
Size: 6"
Season: Year-round
Habitat: Salt- or freshwater wetlands

The secretive Black Rail is a rare, diminutive rail that is difficult to see as it skulks in dense wetland vegetation. It is plump with a short tail and bill and has bright red eyes. The plumage is dark gray-brown above and slate gray below, with white spotting across the back and flanks and a rust patch across the upper shoulders. Both sexes and juveniles are similar in coloration. Black Rails are mostly nocturnal, voicing a ragged *Kik-A-Dow* or a low cooing sound as they forage among grasses for aquatic invertebrates, plants, and seeds. When disturbed they will often run rather than fly. (Illustration shows an adult.)

Clapper Rail,
Rallus longirostris
Family Rallidae (Rails, Coots)
Size: 14"
Season: Year-round
Habitat: Coastal saltwater or brackish marshes, mangrove swamps

Also known as the Marsh Hen, the Clapper Rail is very shy and difficult to see. It lurks through marshy vegetation and usually chooses to walk or swim rather than fly. It forages by probing through mud and grass for a variety of small prey, vocalizing harsh, clattering *Kek-kek-kek* sounds in rapid succession. The Clapper Rail is relatively thin, with a long, slightly decurved bill. The plumage is gray-brown above, with a pale grayish-brown breast and barred flanks. (Illustration shows an adult.)

Sora, *Porzana carolina*
Family Rallidae (Rails, Coots)
Size: 9"
Season: Winter
Habitat: Coastal marshes, meadows

The Sora is a small, short-tailed, chicken-shaped rail with long, thin toes. Its plumage is mottled rusty brown above and grayish below, with white barring along the belly and sides. The head has a black patch between the eye and the yellow, conical bill. The tail is pointed and often cocked up and flicked. The juvenile is pale brown below, with less black on the face. Soras feed along shorelines or at the edges of meadows for snails, insects, and aquatic plants. Their voice is a soft, rising *Ooo-EEP*. Soras are quite tame and are seen more often than other rails. (Illustration shows a breeding adult.)

Common Moorhen,
Gallinula chloropus
Family Rallidae (Rails, Coots)
Size: 14"
Season: Year-round
Habitat: Freshwater ponds and wetlands

Also known as the Common Gallinule, the Common Moorhen is actually a type of rail that behaves more like a duck. It paddles along, bobbing its head up and down as it picks at the water's surface for small aquatic animals, insects, or plants. Having short wings, it is a poor flier, but its very long toes allow it to walk on floating vegetation. It is dark gray overall, with a brownish back, black head, and white areas on the tail and sides. In breeding plumage the forehead shield is deep red and the bill is red with a yellow tip. (Illustration shows a breeding adult.)

Purple Gallinule,
Porphyrio martinica
Family Rallidae (Rails, Coots)
Size: 13"
Season: Summer
Habitat: Freshwater marshes

The Purple Gallinule is a beautifully colored version of the moorhen that behaves more like a duck than a rail. It has a thick, conical bill and long, bright yellow legs and toes. The plumage is rich blue-purple below and on the head, glossy green across the back and wings. The undertail coverts are white. The bill is red with a yellow tip, and its upper base merges with a pale gray-blue forehead shield. The sexes are similar; juveniles are pale below and greenish brown above. Gallinules fly reluctantly, with their legs dangling behind the body. Gallinules walk across floating vegetation and marsh grasses, using their long toes for support as they hunt for aquatic invertebrates, frogs, fish, seeds, and fruit. The voice consists of chickenlike squeaks or clucks. (Illustration shows an adult.)

American Coot, *Fulica americana*
Family Rallidae (Rails, Coots)
Size: 15"
Season: Year-round
Habitat: Wetlands, ponds,
urban lawns, and parks

The American Coot is a rail like the Moorhen but has a plumper body and a thicker head and neck. It is very common and becomes relatively tame in urban areas and parks. To feed, the coot dives for fish, but it will also dabble like a duck or pick food from the ground. The American Coot is dark gray overall, with a black head and a white bill that ends with a dark narrow ring. The white trailing edge of the wings can be seen in flight. The toes are flanked with lobes that enable the coot to walk on water plants and swim efficiently. Juveniles are similar in plumage but are paler. Coots are often seen in very large flocks. (Illustration shows an adult.)

Black-bellied Plover,
Pluvialis squatarola
Family Charadriidae (Plovers)
Size: 11"
Season: Winter
Habitat: Open areas, coastal or inland

The Black-bellied Plover is a relatively large plover with long, pointed wings and a whistling flight call. Like other plovers it feeds by scooting quickly along the ground, stopping suddenly to peck at small prey in the mud or sand, and then scooting along again. The bill is short, black, and thick. In flight there is a distinctive black patch on the axillary feathers. Winter plumage is gray above and paler below, with a white belly. In breeding plumage the Black-bellied Plover develops the sharply contrasting black belly, face, and front of the neck. (Illustration shows a breeding adult, below, and a nonbreeding adult, above.)

Semipalmated Plover,
Charadrius semipalmatus
Family Charadriidae (Plovers)
Size: 7"
Season: Winter
Habitat: Open sand or mudflats,
coastal beaches

The Semipalmated Plover is a small, plump plover with pointed wings, large black eyes, and a relatively large, rounded head. It has a dark brown back and crown, is white below, and has a small, orange bill with a dark tip. The head has dark bands across the eyes and encircling the neck. The legs and feet are yellow. Winter and breeding plumages are similar, with the exception of an all-dark bill and a lighter supercilium in winter. This widespread plover flies in flocks but disperses to feed, when it uses fast running interrupted by sudden stops to probe for invertebrates. The plover's name is derived from the partial webbing at the base of its toes. (Illustration shows a breeding adult.)

Killdeer, *Charadrius vociferus*
Family Charadriidae (Plovers)
Size: 10"
Season: Year-round
Habitat: Inland fields, farmlands, lake
shores, meadows

The Killdeer gets its name from the piercing *Kill-Dee* call, which is often heard before these well-camouflaged plovers are seen. Well adapted to human-altered environments, the Killdeer is quite widespread and gregarious. It has long, pointed wings, a long tail, and a conspicuous double-banded breast. Its upper parts are dark brown, its belly is white, and its head is patterned, with a white supercilium and forehead. The tail is rusty orange with a black tip. In flight there is a noticeable white stripe across the flight feathers. The Killdeer is known for its classic "broken wing" display, which it uses to distract predators from its nest and young. (Illustration shows an adult.)

American Oystercatcher,
Haematopus palliatus
Family Haematopodidae
(Oystercatchers)
Size: 18"
Season: Year-round
Habitat: Coastal beaches, tide pools

The American Oystercatcher is a chunky, short-tailed, and short-winged shorebird with a dark brown back, white belly, and black head. It has a heavy, knifelike, bright red bill, yellow eyes, and stocky, salmon-colored legs. In flight there is a distinct white bar across the secondary feathers. Oystercatchers follow the tidal pattern, foraging at low tide and roosting at high tide in groups with other shorebirds and gulls. They use their bill to pry shellfish—including oysters—from rocks or to probe for worms. They also use their bill to jam open bivalves and devour the flesh. The voice is a loud, piping call. (Illustration shows an adult.)

Black-necked Stilt,
Himantopus mexicanus
Family Recurvirostridae
(Avocets, Stilts)
Size: 14"
Season: Summer
Habitat: Shallow wetlands,
marshes, lagoons

The Black-necked Stilt literally looks like a tiny body on stilts. It has extremely long, delicate red legs and a thin, straight, needlelike black bill. Wings and mantle are black, and the underparts and tail are white. The head is dark above, with a white patch above the eyes. The female has a slightly lighter, brownish back. In flight the long legs dangle behind the bird. To forage it strides along to pick small prey from the water or vegetation, and it may voice a strident, barking *Kek!* when alarmed. Stilts are also known to perform the "broken wing" or "broken leg" display to distract predators from their nests and young. (Illustration shows an adult male.)

Spotted Sandpiper,
Actitus macularius
Family Scolopacidae
(Sandpipers, Phalaropes)
Size: 7.5"
Season: Winter
Habitat: Streamsides, edges of lakes and ponds

The solitary Spotted Sandpiper is known for its exaggerated, constant bobbing motion. It has a compact body, a long tail, a short neck, and short legs. The plumage is brown above and light below, with a white shoulder patch. There is a white eye ring and superciliary stripe above the dark eye line. In breeding plumage it develops heavy spotting from the chin to lower flanks and barring on the back. The bill is orange with a dark tip. Spotted Sandpipers have short wings, and in flight the thin white stripe on the upper wing can be seen. To forage they teeter about, picking small water prey and insects from the shoreline. (Illustration shows a breeding adult.)

Greater Yellowlegs,
Tringa melanoleuca
Family Scolopacidae
(Sandpipers, Phalaropes)
Size: 14"
Season: Winter
Habitat: Salt- or freshwater marshes

The Greater Yellowlegs is sometimes called the "telltale" bird, as the sentinel of a flock raises alarm when danger is near, flying off and circling to return. It has long, bright yellow legs, a long neck, a dark, slightly upturned bill, and white eye rings. Its upperparts are dark gray and mottled; its underparts are white, with barring on the flanks. In breeding plumage the barring is noticeably darker and more extensive. To feed, the Greater Yellowlegs strides forward actively to pick small aquatic prey from the water or to chase fish. The Lesser Yellowlegs is similar but smaller. (Illustration shows a nonbreeding adult.)

Willet, *Tringa semipalmatus*
Family Scolopacidae
(Sandpipers, Phalaropes)
Size: 15"
Season: Year-round
Habitat: Salt- or freshwater wetlands

The Willet is a heavy shorebird with a stout bill and conspicuous black-and-white wing markings in flight. It has overall mocha-brown plumage above and pale below, with extensive mottling in the breeding season. It has white lores and eye rings, and its plain gray legs are thick and sturdy. Willets are found singly or in scattered flocks and pick or probe for crabs, crustaceans, and worms in the mud and sand. The voice, a loud *Wil-Let,* is often uttered in flight. (Illustration shows a nonbreeding adult.)

Marbled Godwit,
Limosa fedoa
Family Scolopacidae
(Sandpipers, Phalaropes)
Size: 18"
Season: Winter
Habitat: Coastal beaches, mudflats, marshes

As its name suggests, the Marbled Godwit is marbled, or barred, with dark across its buff-colored body, although the undersides lack marbling in winter plumage. The long, pinkish bill has a slight upcurved portion at the tip, where it becomes dark in color. The legs are dark, and the underwing is a rich cinnamon color. There is a light superciliary stripe above a dark eye line. Marbled Godwits move about with slow, steady progress and probe in shallow water to feed on polychaete worms and crustaceans. The call is a loud *god-WIT.* (Illustration shows a nonbreeding adult.)

Ruddy Turnstone,
Arenaria interpres
Family Scolopacidae
(Sandpipers, Phalaropes)
Size: 9.5"
Season: Winter
Habitat: Wide variety of shoreline
habitats, from rocky intertidal to beaches and mudflats

The gregarious and frenetic Ruddy Turnstone is a chunky, short-legged shorebird with a short, wedge-shaped bill. The breeding adult has ruddy and black upperparts, a white belly, and a complex pattern of black and white on the head. The nonbreeding bird is pale brown and black above, with drab head markings. The stubby legs are orange. In flight the bird is white below and strongly patterned light and dark above. Turnstones bustle about constantly to pick, pry, or probe for almost any food item. Indeed, it will "turn stones" to search for prey. (Illustration shows a breeding adult, below, and a nonbreeding adult, above.)

Red Knot, *Calidris canutus*
Family Scolopacidae
(Sandpipers, Phalaropes)
Size: 10.5"
Season: Winter
Habitat: Coastal beaches and mudflats

The Red Knot is a compact, short-legged shorebird with a slightly downcurved bill. In breeding plumage it has a rufous body with a grayish back and wings. Nonbreeding plumage is mottled gray-brown above and pale below, with light streaking. The dark bill is about the length of the head. The long, pointed wings, which are gray underneath, can be seen in flight. It forages by probing and picking in the mud or sand for a variety of small prey. Red Knots often form tight flocks while roosting and feeding. (Illustration shows a breeding adult, below, and a nonbreeding adult, above.)

Sanderling, *Calidris alba*
Family Scolopacidae
(Sandpipers, Phalaropes)
Size: 8"
Season: Winter
Habitat: Coastal beaches, mudflats

The Sanderling is a small, active, squat sandpiper with a short bill and legs. This common shorebird runs back and forth, following the incoming and outgoing surf and grabbing invertebrates exposed by the waves. In nonbreeding plumage it is very pale above and white below, which contrasts with its black legs and bill. There is a distinct black shoulder and leading edge on the wing. Females in breeding plumage are speckled brown above, while males develop rufous on the back, head, and neck. A white wing stripe on the upper wing can be seen in flight. Sanderlings may form large flocks while foraging and even larger flocks while roosting. (Illustration shows a nonbreeding adult.)

Western Sandpiper,
Calidris mauri
Family Scolopacidae
(Sandpipers, Phalaropes)
Size: 6.5"
Season: Winter
Habitat: Saltwater and freshwater
wetlands, mudflats, coastal beaches

The Western Sandpiper is one of the "peeps," or very small sandpipers. It has black legs and a relatively long black bill that droops slightly. In winter it is pale gray-brown above and white below. In breeding plumage there is rufous on the scapulars and face and much darker streaking on the breast and back. A thin white stripe on the upper wing is visible in flight, along with a white rump with a dark central stripe. Western Sandpipers feed in shallow water or at the tide line, probing or picking invertebrates and insects. They often form rather large flocks. (Illustration shows a breeding adult, below, and a nonbreeding adult, above.)

Dunlin, *Calidris alpina*
Family Scolopacidae
(Sandpipers, Phalaropes)
Size: 8.5"
Season: Winter
Habitat: Coastal beaches, mudflats

The name "Dunlin" comes from the word dun, which means a dull gray-brown color and which describes this bird's winter plumage. It is a rather small sandpiper with a long bill that droops down at the tip. In breeding plumage there is a black belly patch and rufous tones on the back. A white wing stripe on the upper wing and a white rump separated by a central dark line can be seen in flight. Dunlins form huge flocks, swirling and circling in unison. To feed, they walk steadily through shallow waters, probing and picking crustaceans and other invertebrates. (Illustration shows a breeding adult, below, and a nonbreeding adult, above.)

American Woodcock,

Scolopax minor
Family Scolopacidae
(Sandpipers, Phalaropes)
Size: 11"
Season: Year-round
Habitat: Moist fields, woodland edges with brush

The American Woodcock is a reclusive shorebird of upland woods and fields. It has a plump body, large head, long bill, and stubby tail; the legs are short. Plumage is mottled gray above, with distinct, paler gray stripes down the sides of the back; undersides are plain buff to pale orange. The head has a dark crown with transverse buff stripes and large black eyes set high up on the face. Woodcocks are mostly active at night or dusk, probing soft soils for earthworms and insects. The voice is a blunt, nasal sound, and the birds produce a whistling noise in flight from air passing through their thin outer primary feathers. (Illustration shows an adult.)

Bonaparte's Gull,
Chroicocephalus philadelphia
Family Laridae (Gulls, Terns)
Size: 13"
Season: Winter
Habitat: Coastal in winter,
inland during migration

Bonaparte's Gull is a small gull named for the American ornithologist who was related to Napoleon. It is agile and ternlike in flight, skimming low over the water to snatch fish. It has a thin, sharp, black bill and red legs. Plumage in breeding season includes a black head that contrasts with its white body and light gray back and wings. The primaries form a white triangle against the dark trailing edge when the gull is in flight. The nonbreeding adult has a mostly white head, with a black eye and small dark spots around the ear. A solitary gull, the Bonaparte does not form large flocks. It builds nests made of sticks in evergreen trees. (Illustration shows a breeding adult, below, and a nonbreeding adult, above.)

Laughing Gull,
Leucophaeus atricilla
Family Laridae (Gulls, Terns)
Size: 16"
Season: Year-round
Habitat: Coastal beaches and marshes,
urban environments, pastures

The Laughing Gull is so named because of its loud, often incessant, laughing squawk. Social and uninhibited, it is a relatively thin, medium-size gull with long, pointed wings. The breeding adult has a black head with white eye arcs and a dark red bill. Upperparts are dark gray, underparts are white, and wing tips are black with small white dots at the ends. The nonbreeding adult has a white head with faint dark smudging behind the eye. Laughing Gulls eat crabs, fish, and worms and will steal from other birds or even scavenge from humans for food. (Illustration shows a breeding adult, below, and a nonbreeding adult, above.)

Ring-billed Gull,
Larus delewarensis
Family Laridae (Gulls, Terns)
Size: 18″
Season: Winter
Habitat: From coast to inland lakes and ponds, parking lots

The widespread Ring-billed Gull is common and quite tame. It is a relatively small gull with a rounded, white head and a yellow bill with a dark subterminal ring. It has a pale gray back with black primaries tipped with white and white underparts. The eyes are pale yellow; the legs are yellow as well. The nonbreeding adult has faint streaking on the nape and around the eye. Ring-billed Gulls feed from the water or on the ground, taking a wide variety of foodstuffs, and may scavenge in urban areas and dumps. (Illustration shows a nonbreeding adult.)

Herring Gull, *Larus argentatus*
Family Laridae (Gulls, Terns)
Size: 25″
Season: Year-round along the coast; winter inland
Habitat: Mainly coastal but may travel inland; beaches, harbors, fields

The widespread Herring Gull occurs across the North American continent. It is a large, relatively thin, and white-headed gull with a pale gray back and white underparts. The bill is thick and yellow with a reddish spot at the tip of the lower mandible. The primaries are black with white-spotted tips. The nonbreeding adult has brown streaking across the nape and neck. The gull's legs are pink, and the eyes are pale yellow to ivory colored. The Herring Gull is an opportunistic feeder, eating fish, worms, crumbs, and trash. It is known to drop shellfish from the air to crack open the shells. (Illustration shows a breeding adult, below, and a nonbreeding adult, above.)

Great Black-backed Gull,
Larus marinus
Family Laridae (Gulls, Terns)
Size: 29"
Season: Winter
Habitat: Coastal beaches, rocky shores, estuaries

The Great Black-backed Gull is the largest gull worldwide, with a proportionately large head and bill. Plumage is white with a dark, slate gray back and wings marked with white-edged tertials and secondaries and tips of the outer primaries. The bill is yellow with a red spot on the lower mandible, and the legs are pink. Adults in winter plumage have minimal gray streaking on the top part of the head, and juveniles show extensive mottling and spotting on the back and breast. The gulls feed and scavenge on almost anything edible, including fish, mammals, birds, eggs, and invertebrates, and they dominate other species in mixed flocks. They will sometimes drop food items from the air onto hard surfaces to crack or kill them. (Illustration shows a breeding adult.)

Least Tern,
Sternula antillarum
Family Laridae (Gulls, Terns)
Size: 9"
Season: Summer
Habitat: Sandy coastal shores

The Least Tern is the smallest North American tern and the only tern with a yellow bill and legs. It has a black cap and white forehead patch and is pale gray above and white below. The tail is forked, and the bill is tipped with black. Nonbreeding adults have a dark bill and increased white on the front of the cap. In flight the wings are relatively narrow, and there is a black bar on the outer primaries. Least Terns often hover over the water before plunge-diving to catch small fish. They also pick worms and insects from the ground. This environmentally sensitive bird was once threatened by development of its sandy coastal breeding grounds. (Illustration shows a breeding adult.)

Forster's Tern,
Sterna forsteri
Family Laridae (Gulls, Terns)
Size: 14"
Season: Winter
Habitat: Coastal areas, lakes, marshes

The Forster's Tern is a medium-size tern with no crest and a relatively long, pointed orange bill with a black tip. Breeding plumage is very pale gray above and white below, with a forked white tail and very light primaries. The head has a black cap, and the short legs are red. Nonbreeding adults have darker primaries, a black ear patch in place of the cap, and a black bill. Forster's Terns display swallowlike flight, with narrow pointed wings, and they plunge-dive for fish. They voice short, harsh, one-syllable calls. (Illustration shows a nonbreeding adult, above, and breeding adult, below.)

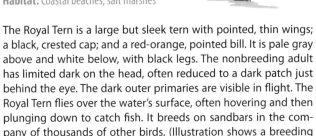

Royal Tern,
Thalasseus maxima
Family Laridae (Gulls, Terns)
Size: 20"
Season: Year-round
Habitat: Coastal beaches, salt marshes

The Royal Tern is a large but sleek tern with pointed, thin wings; a black, crested cap; and a red-orange, pointed bill. It is pale gray above and white below, with black legs. The nonbreeding adult has limited dark on the head, often reduced to a dark patch just behind the eye. The dark outer primaries are visible in flight. The Royal Tern flies over the water's surface, often hovering and then plunging down to catch fish. It breeds on sandbars in the company of thousands of other birds. (Illustration shows a breeding adult, below, and a nonbreeding adult, above.)

Sandwich Tern,

Thalasseus sandvicensis
Family Laridae (Gulls, Terns)
Size: 15"
Season: Summer
Habitat: Coastal bays, estuaries, offshore waters, islands

The Sandwich Tern is a streamlined, slender seabird that is similar in shape to the Royal Tern but quite a bit smaller. It has a long, thin, black bill with a pointed yellow tip, forked wings, short black legs, and a ragged black crest. Plumage is pale, pearly gray above and white below, with darker tips to the primaries (more visible in flight). Nonbreeding adults show white on the front half of the crown. Sandwich Terns plunge-dive into ocean waters for fish, squid, or shrimp. They are often seen associating with Royal Terns, especially on breeding grounds. (Illustration shows a breeding adult, below, and a nonbreeding adult, above.)

Caspian Tern, *Sterna caspia*

Family Laridae (Gulls, Terns)
Size: 21"
Season: Winter
Habitat: Coastal and inland lakes and rivers

The Caspian Tern is a very large, thick-necked tern—the size of a big gull. It has a pointed, rich red bill that is dark at the tip and has a black cap on its head. Upperparts are very pale gray; underparts are white. The primary feathers are pale gray above and tipped with dark on the underside. The legs are short and black. Nonbreeding adults have pale streaks through the cap. In flight the Caspian Tern uses ponderous, shallow wing beats and is less agile than smaller terns. It flies above the water's surface searching for prey, plunging headfirst to snatch small fish, and may rob food from other birds. Voice is a harsh *Craw!* (Illustration shows a breeding adult.)

Black Skimmer,
Rynchops niger
Family Laridae (Gulls, Terns)
Size: 18"
Season: Year-round
Habitat: Coastal bays, estuaries, or inland freshwater rivers and lakes

The Black Skimmer has a unique bill in which the lower mandible is substantially longer than the upper. The red bill is also thick at the base and knife-thin toward the end. This construction aids in foraging as the bird flies just above the water's surface, wings held above the body, with the mouth open and the lower mandible cutting a furrow through the water. When it encounters something solid, the mouth slams shut and, hopefully, the bird acquires a fish. Plumage is black on the back, wings, and crown and white below. The tiny legs are red. Nonbreeding adults have a white nape, contiguous with the white of the body. (Illustration shows a breeding adult.)

Rock Pigeon, *Columba livia*
Family Columbidae (Pigeons, Doves)
Size: 12"
Season: Year-round
Habitat: Urban areas, farmland

The Rock Pigeon (also known as the Rock Dove) is the common pigeon seen in almost every urban area across the continent. Introduced from Europe, where they inhabit rocky cliffs, Rock Pigeons here have adapted to city life, and domestication has supplied a huge variety of plumage colors and patterns. The original, wild version is a stocky gray bird with a darker head and neck and green to purple iridescence along the sides of the neck. The eyes are bright red, and the bill has a fleshy white cere on the base of the upper mandible. There are two dark bars across the back when the wings are folded; the rump is white, and the tail has a dark terminal band. Variants range from white to brown to black, with many pattern combinations. (Illustration shows an adult.)

Eurasian Collared-Dove,

Streptopelia decaocto
Family Columbidae (Pigeons, Doves)
Size: 12.5"
Season: Year-round
Habitat: Human-altered
environments, pastures, rooftops

The Eurasian Collared-Dove was introduced to the United States from Europe and is gradually increasing its numbers here. It is a stocky, fairly large dove with a squarish tail. Plumage is light brown-gray overall, with darker primaries, white along the outer edges of the tail, and a contrasting black streak around the nape. The eyes are red, and the bill is black. It is very similar in appearance to the smaller, paler Ringed Turtle-Dove. The dove eats mainly seeds and grain. (Illustration shows an adult.)

Mourning Dove,

Zenaida macroura
Family Columbidae (Pigeons, Doves)
Size: 12"
Season: Year-round
Habitat: Open brushy areas,
urban areas

The common Mourning Dove is a sleek, long-tailed dove with a thin neck; a small, rounded head; and large, black eyes. Underneath it is pale gray-brown and darker above, with some iridescence to feathers on the neck. There are clear, black spots on the tertials and some coverts, and there's a dark spot on the upper neck below the eyes. The pointed tail is edged with a white band. The Mourning Dove pecks on the ground for seeds and grains and walks with quick, short steps while bobbing its head. Flight is strong and direct, and the wings create a whistle as the bird takes off. Its voice is a mournful, owl-like cooing. Mourning Doves are solitary or live in small groups, but they may form large flocks where food is abundant. (Illustration shows an adult.)

Yellow-billed Cuckoo,

Coccyzus americanus
Family Cuculidae (Cuckoos)
Size: 12"
Season: Summer
Habitat: Streamsides, swamps,
a variety of woodlands

Like other cuckoos, the Yellow-billed Cuckoo is secretive and shy. It hides in vegetation, where it picks insects, caterpillars, and fruit from trees. It is brown above, with rufous flight feathers and crisp white below. The bill is yellow with black along the top ridge. The tail is long and gradated, with large white spots on the underside. (Illustration shows an adult.)

Barn Owl, *Tyto alba*
Family Tytonidae (Barn Owls)
Size: 23"
Season: Year-round
Habitat: Barns, farmland, open areas
with mature trees

The Barn Owl is a large-headed, pale owl with small dark eyes, a heart-shaped facial disk, and long, feathered legs. The wings, back, tail, and crown are light rusty brown with light gray smudging and small white dots. The underside, face, and underwing linings are white, with spots of rust on the breast. Females are usually darker than males, with more color and spotting across the breast and sides. The facial disk is enclosed by a thin line of darker feathers. Barn Owls are nocturnal hunters for rodents. Its voice is a haunting, raspy *Screeee!* (Illustration shows an adult male.)

Eastern Screech-Owl,

Megascops asio
Family Strigidae (Typical Owls)
Size: 8.5"
Season: Year-round
Habitat: Wooded areas or parks, places where cavity-bearing trees exist

The Eastern Screech Owl is a small, eared owl with a big head, short tail, and bright yellow eyes. The highly camouflaged plumage ranges from reddish to brown to gray, depending on the region, but the red form is most common in the East. It is darker above, streaked and barred below. The ear tufts may be drawn back to give the appearance of a rounded head, and the bill is grayish green tipped with white. White spots on the margins of the coverts and scapulars create two white bars on the folded wing. It is a nocturnal bird, hunting during the night for small mammals, insects, or fish. Its voice is a descending, whistling call or a rapid staccato of one pitch. (Illustration shows a red morph adult.)

Great Horned Owl,

Bubo virginianus
Family Strigidae (Typical Owls)
Size: 22"
Season: Year-round
Habitat: Almost any environment; forests to plains to urban areas

Found throughout North America, the Great Horned Owl is a large, strong owl with an obvious facial disk and sharp, long talons. Plumage is variable. Eastern forms are brown overall with heavy barring, a rust-colored face, and a white chin patch. The prominent ear tufts give the owl its name, and the eyes are large and yellow. The Great Horned Owl has exceptional hearing and sight. It feeds at night, perching on branches or posts, then swooping down on silent wings to catch birds, snakes, or mammals up to the size of a cat. Its voice is a low *Hoo-Hoo-Hoo*. (Illustration shows an adult.)

Barred Owl,

Strix varia
Family Strigidae (Typical Owls)
Size: 21"
Season: Year-round
Habitat: Wooded swamps,
upland forests

The Barred Owl is a large, compact owl with a short tail and wings, a rounded head, and big, dark eyes. It lacks the ear tufts seen on the Great Horned Owl and has comparatively small talons. Plumage is gray-brown overall with dark barring on the neck and breast, turning to streaking on the belly and flanks. It swoops from its perch to catch small rodents, frogs, or snakes. Its voice, often heard during the day, is a hooting *Who-cooks-for-you* or a kind of bark. Barred Owls nest in tree cavities vacated by other species. (Illustration shows an adult.)

Common Nighthawk,

Chordeiles minor
Family Caprimulgidae
(Nightjars, Nighthawks)
Size: 9"
Season: Summer
Habitat: Forests, marshes, plains,
urban areas

The Common Nighthawk is primarily nocturnal but may be seen flying during the day and evening hours, catching insects on the wing with bounding flight. It is cryptically mottled gray, brown, and black, with strong barring on an otherwise pale underside. In the male a white breast band is evident. The tail is long and slightly notched, and the wings are long and pointed, extending past the tail in the perched bird. In flight there is a distinct white patch on both sides of the wings. During the day the Common Nighthawk is usually seen roosting on posts or branches with its eyes closed. Its voice is a short, nasal, buzzing sound. (Illustration shows an adult male.)

Chuck-will's-widow,
Caprimulgus carolinensis
Family Caprimulgidae (Nightjars, Nighthawks)
Size: 12"
Season: Summer
Habitat: Woodland areas with clearings

Chuck-will's-widow is a highly camouflaged, fairly large nightjar with a fat head; big, dark eyes; and a tiny bill. The body is thick and broad around the midsection, giving the bird a hunched appearance. It is overall rusty or brown-gray, spotted and streaked with black. There are pale edges to the scapulars and a pale chin stripe above the dark breast. The tail is long and projects beyond the primaries. In flight the long, pointed wings and white on the outer tail feathers in the male can be seen. Chuck-will's-widow is nocturnal, feeding at night by springing from its perch or the ground to catch flying insects. During the day it roosts on the ground or in trees with its eyes closed. Its voice is somewhat like its name: *Chuck-Wil-Wi-Dow.* (Illustration shows an adult.)

Chimney Swift,
Chaetura pelagica
Family Apodidae (Swifts)
Size: 5"
Season: Summer
Habitat: Woods, scrub, swamps, urban areas

The gregarious Chimney Swift is unrelated to the swallows but similar in shape. Its body is like a fat torpedo, with a very short tail and long, pointed, bowed wings that bend close to the body. It is dark brown overall, slightly paler underneath and at the chin. Constantly on the wing, it catches insects in flight with quick wing beats and fast glides. It never perches, roosting at night on vertical cliffs, in trees, or in chimneys. Its voice is a quick chattering uttered in flight. (Illustration shows an adult.)

Ruby-throated Hummingbird,
Archilochus colubris
Family Trochilidae (Hummingbirds)
Size: 3.5"
Season: Summer
Habitat: Gardens and other areas with flowering plants, urban feeders

The Ruby-throated Hummingbird is a small, delicate bird able to hover on wings that beat at a blinding speed. The bird uses its long, needlelike bill to probe deep into flowers to lap up the nectar. Its body is white below and green above, and the feet are tiny. Males have a dark green crown and an iridescent red throat, or gorget. Females lack the colored gorget and have a light green crown and white-tipped tail feathers. Their behavior is typical of hummingbirds, hovering and buzzing from flower to flower, emitting chits and squeaks. Most of these birds migrate across the Gulf of Mexico to South America in winter. (Illustration shows an adult male, below, and a female, above.)

Belted Kingfisher,
Megaceryle alcyon
Family Alcedinidae (Kingfishers)
Size: 13"
Season: Year-round
Habitat: Creeks, lakes, sheltered coastline

The widespread but solitary Belted Kingfisher is a stocky, large-headed bird with a long, powerful bill and a shaggy crest. It is grayish blue-green above and white below, with a thick blue band across the breast and white dotting on the back. There are white spots at the lores. The female has an extra breast band of rufous and is rufous along the flanks. Belted Kingfishers feed by springing from a perch along the water's edge or hovering above the water and then plunging headfirst to snatch fish, frogs, or tadpoles. Flight is uneven, and its voice is a raspy, rattling sound. (Illustration shows an adult female.)

Red-headed Woodpecker,
Melanerpes erythrocephalus
Family Picidae (Woodpeckers)
Size: 9"
Season: Year-round
Habitat: Woodlands, areas with standing dead trees, suburbs

The Red-headed Woodpecker has a striking bright red head and a powerful tapered bill. It is black above, with a large patch of white across the lower back and secondaries, and is white below. Juveniles have a pale brown head and incomplete white back patch. In all woodpeckers the tail is very stiff, with sharp tips that help support the bird while it clings to a tree trunk. To feed, it pecks at bark for insects but may also fly out to snatch its prey in midair. Red-headed Woodpeckers will also take and store nuts in tree cavities for winter. This species has been losing nesting cavities since the introduction of the European Starling. (Illustration shows an adult.)

Red-bellied Woodpecker,
Melanerpes carolinus
Family Picidae (Woodpeckers)
Size: 9"
Season: Year-round
Habitat: Woodlands, wooded swamps, parks, urban areas

The Red-bellied Woodpecker is a fairly common, large-billed woodpecker with extensively barred back and wings. The underparts are pale buff, with a barely discernable hint of rose on the belly that gives the bird its name. The crown and nape are reddish orange. Females lack the red crown, and juveniles have an entirely gray head. Like all woodpeckers, the Red-bellied Woodpecker has two toes pointing forward and two toes pointing back to allow a secure grip on tree trunks as it pecks away bark to find insects. It also feeds on nuts and oranges. Flight is undulating wing beats and glides. (Illustration shows an adult male.)

Downy Woodpecker,

Picoides pubescens
Family Picidae (Woodpeckers)
Size: 6.5"
Season: Year-round
Habitat: Woodlands, parks,
urban areas, streamsides

The Downy Woodpecker is a tiny woodpecker with a small bill and a relatively large head. It is white underneath with no barring, has black wings barred with white, and has a patch of white on the back. The head is boldly patterned white and black, and the male sports a red nape patch. The base of the bill joins the head with fluffy nasal tufts. Juveniles may show some red on the forehead and crown. It forages for berries and insects in the bark and among the smaller twigs of trees. The very similar Hairy Woodpecker is larger, with a longer bill and more aggressive foraging behavior, sticking to larger branches and not clinging to twigs. (Illustration shows an adult male.)

Red-cockaded Woodpecker,

Picoides borealis
Family Picidae (Woodpeckers)
Size: 8.5"
Season: Year-round
Habitat: Old growth pine forests

The Red-cockaded Woodpecker nests only in mature pine trees and is therefore rare and declining in numbers as it loses its habitat to development. It is a thin-looking, medium-size woodpecker with a long tail. Plumage is barred with black and white on the back and white beneath, with numerous spots and bars. The patterned head has a large white cheek patch and nasal tufts. The red cockade spot at the back of the crown on the male is rarely apparent in the field. Juveniles show a red forehead spot. Red-cockaded Woodpeckers form small groups called clans that forage together, pecking into tree bark for beetles and other insects. (Illustration shows an adult male.)

Pileated Woodpecker,
Dryocopus pileatus
Family Picidae (Woodpeckers)
Size: 16.5"
Season: Year-round
Habitat: Old-growth forests,
urban areas with large trees

The Pileated Woodpecker is North America's largest woodpecker except for the probably extinct Ivory-billed Woodpecker. It is very large and powerful, with a long neck and a crest. The body is all black with a white base to the primaries, which are mostly covered in the folded wing. The head is boldly patterned black and white, with a bright red crest that is limited on the female. The male has a red malar patch instead of the black of the female. In flight the contrasting white wing lining can be seen. The Pileated Woodpecker chips away chunks of bark to uncover ants and beetles but will feed on berries during winter. Its voice is a high-pitched, uneven, and resounding *Wok-wok-wok.* (Illustration shows an adult male.)

Northern Flicker,
Colaptes auratus
Family Picidae (Woodpeckers)
Size: 12.5"
Season: Year-round
Habitat: A variety of habitats,
including suburbs and parks

The common Northern Flicker is a large, long-tailed woodpecker often seen foraging on the ground for ants and other small insects. It is barred brown and black across the back and buff with black spotting below. The head is brown with a gray nape and crown and a small red patch behind the head. On the upper breast is a prominent half-circle of black, and the male has a black patch at the malar region. Flight is undulating and shows the golden yellow wing lining and white rump. The flicker's voice is a loud, sharp *Keee,* and it will sometimes drum its bill repeatedly at objects, like a jackhammer. (Illustration shows an adult male.)

PASSERINES

Eastern Wood-Pewee,
Contopus virens
Family Tyrannidae
(Tyrant Flycatchers)
Size: 6.25"
Season: Summer
Habitat: Woodland edges,
canyons, creeksides

The Eastern Wood-Pewee is a large-headed, thick-necked fly-catcher with drab plumage overall. It is brownish gray or olive-gray, with pale whitish or dusky underparts and gray sides that meet at the breast. A very slight eye ring surrounds the dark eye; the bill is thin and pointed and has a pale lower mandible. There are thin wing bars along the coverts and edges of the tertials. It is nearly identical to the Western Wood-Pewee, but the ranges do not normally overlap. Eastern Wood-Pewees flycatch for insects, starting from a high perch and then returning to the same spot. The voice is composed of shrill, high-pitched *Pee-Wee* notes. (Illustration shows an adult.)

Acadian Flycatcher,
Empidonax virescens
Family Tyrannidae (Tyrant Flycatchers)
Size: 6"
Season: Summer
Habitat: Wooded riparian areas

The Acadian Flycatcher is a member of the sometimes-confusing Empidonax group, which breeds throughout the southeastern United States. It has a relatively long, robust bill, long wings, and a thin eye ring, and the hind crown often shows a slight peak. Plumage is olive green above and whitish below, with variable amounts of pale yellow wash on the lower belly and a faint greenish breast band. The wings are dark, with pale wing bars and edges to the tertials. Both sexes and juveniles are similar. Acadian Flycatchers flycatch for insects within the tree canopy and may also eat berries. The voice is a sharp, high-pitched *Peet-SEE,* rising on the second syllable. (Illustration shows an adult.)

Eastern Phoebe,
Sayornis phoebe
Family Tyrannidae
(Tyrant Flycatchers)
Size: 7"
Season: Year-round
Habitat: Brushy streamsides

The Eastern Phoebe is a compact, large-headed flycatcher with a thin, pointed bill and a long tail that it habitually pumps up and down. Plumage is grayish across the back, wings, tail, and head, with darker areas on the face and crown. The underparts are white, sometimes washed with pale yellow on the belly, with a bit of gray extending onto the sides of the breast. The wing bars are quite dull, and there is no distinct eye ring. Sexes are similar; juveniles show more yellow on the underparts. Eastern Phoebes flycatch for insects from branch tips or fence wires. The voice sounds somewhat like its name, *Fee-Bee,* or is a series of chattering *Sit* notes. (Illustration shows an adult.)

Great Crested Flycatcher,
Myiarchus crinitus
Family Tyrannidae (Tyrant Flycatchers)
Size: 8.5"
Season: Summer
Habitat: Open woodlands and scrub, urban areas

The Great Crested Flycatcher is a large flycatcher with a proportionately large head and a full crest. The upperparts and head are olive-brown; the throat and breast are gray with a bright yellow belly. The primaries and tail show rufous color, while the margins to the tertials and coverts are white. Both sexes and juveniles have similar plumage. In flight the yellow wing linings and rufous tail can be seen. The flycatcher feeds by flying from perch to perch, catching insects in flight. It is often seen erecting its crown feathers and bobbing its head. The voice is a high-pitched, whistling *Wheeeerup!* (Illustration shows an adult.)

Eastern Kingbird,
Tyrannus tyrannus
Family Tyrannidae
(Tyrant Flycatchers)
Size: 8.5"
Season: Summer
Habitat: Open woodlands, agricultural and rural areas

The Eastern Kingbird is a slender, medium-size flycatcher. Its upperparts are bluish black, and its underparts are white with a pale gray breast. The dark head cap contrasts with the white lower half of the face. The tail is black with a white terminal band. It flies with shallow wing beats on wings that are mostly dark and pointed. Eastern Kingbirds perch on wires, treetops, or posts and take flight to capture insects on the wing. The voice is a distinctive series of very high-pitched, sputtering, zippy *Psit* notes. (Illustration shows an adult.)

Loggerhead Shrike,
Lanius ludovicianus
Family Laniidae (Shrikes)
Size: 9.5"
Season: Year-round
Habitat: Open, dry country with available perches, including branches, wires, and posts

The solitary Loggerhead Shrike is raptorlike in its feeding habits. It captures large insects, small mammals, or birds and impales them on thorny barbs before tearing them apart to feed. It is a compact, large-headed bird with a short, thick, slightly hooked bill. Its upperparts are gray, its underparts pale. The wings are black with white patches at the base of the primaries and upper coverts. The tail is black and edged with white. There is a black mask on the head from the base of the bill to the ear area. Juveniles show a finely barred breast. The shrike's flight is composed of quick wing beats and swooping glides. (Illustration shows an adult.)

White-eyed Vireo,
Vireo griseus
Family Vireonidae (Vireos)
Size: 5"
Season: Year-round
Habitat: Dense woodlands, thickets, shrubs

The White-eyed Vireo is a small, chunky vireo with a relatively large head and a short bill. It is grayish olive green above and pale gray below, tinged with yellow on the flanks and undertail coverts. The head is grayish with conspicuous yellow "spectacles," or a combined lores and eye ring area. The large eye is white. On the wings are two white wing bars. Juveniles have a darker eye than that of adults. White-eyed Vireos glean insects, spiders, and berries from dense vegetation. (Illustration shows an adult.)

Yellow-throated Vireo,

Vireo flavifrons
Family Vireonidae (Vireos)
Size: 5.5"
Season: Summer
Habitat: High canopy in mature, moist, mixed woodlands

The Yellow-throated Vireo is a compact vireo with a short tail. It has olive and gray upperparts with a bright yellow chin and breast, fading to a white belly and undertail region. Yellow "spectacles" encircle the dark eyes. There are two distinct white wing bars on the wing coverts. The vireo gleans insects and berries from leaves high in the canopy. (Illustration shows an adult.)

Blue-headed Vireo,

Vireo solitarius
Family Vireonidae (Vireos)
Size: 5.5"
Season: Winter on the Coastal Plain, summer in the west
Habitat: Woodland, urban areas with trees

The Blue-headed Vireo was once grouped with the Plumbeous and Cassin's Vireos as one species, the Solitary Vireo. It is olive-gray above and white below, tinged with yellow on the sides and flanks. The head is blue-gray, with white "spectacles" and a white chin. There are two white or pale yellow wing bars on the wing coverts. The vireo gleans insects and berries in the upper tree canopies. The voice consists of short, high-pitched phrases. (Illustration shows an adult.)

Red-eyed Vireo,
Vireo olivaceus
Family Vireonidae (Vireos)
Size: 6"
Season: Summer
Habitat: Areas of dense
vegetation, mature deciduous forest

The Red-eyed Vireo is a sluggish, slow-moving bird that haunts the upper tree canopy picking out insects and berries. Its head appears rather flat, and its tail is short. It is light olive green above and white below, with a yellow wash across the breast, flanks, and undertail coverts. It has dark eye lines, white eyebrows, and a grayish crown. The eyes are red, and the bill is fairly large with a hooked tip. The voice is a repetitive, incessant song in single phrases. (Illustration shows an adult.)

Blue Jay,
Cyanocitta cristata
Family Corvidae
(Jays, Crows)
Size: 11"
Season: Year-round
Habitat: Woodlands, rural
and urban areas

The solitary Blue Jay is a sturdy, crested jay. It is bright blue above and white below, with a thick, tapered black bill. There is a white patch around the eye to the chin, bordered by a thin black "necklace" extending to the back of the nape. It has a conspicuous white wing bar and dark barring on wings and tail. In flight the white outer edges of the tail are visible as the jay alternates shallow wing beats with glides. Omnivorous, the Blue Jay eats just about anything, especially acorns, nuts, fruits, insects, and small vertebrates. It is a raucous and noisy bird and quite bold. Sometimes it mimics the calls of birds of prey. (Illustration shows an adult.)

American Crow,
Corvus brachyrhynchos
Family Corvidae (Jays, Crows)
Size: 17.5"
Season: Year-round
Habitat: Open woodlands,
pastures, rural fields, dumps

The American Crow is a widespread corvid found across the continent. Known for its familiar, loud, grating *Caw, caw* vocalization, the crow is a large, stocky bird with a short, rounded tail, broad wings, and a thick, powerful bill. Plumage is glistening black overall, in all stages. It will eat almost anything, often forming loose flocks with other crows. The similar Fish Crow is virtually identical to the American Crow but smaller and glossier overall; it prefers to forage on fish and crustaceans. (Illustration shows an adult American Crow.)

Purple Martin,
Progne subis
Family Hirundinidae (Swallows)
Size: 8"
Season: Summer
Habitat: Marshes, open water,
agricultural areas

The Purple Martin is the largest North American swallow. It has long, pointed wings, a streamlined body, and a forked tail. The bill is very short and broad at the base. The male is dark overall, with a blackish blue sheen across the back and head. The female is paler overall, with sooty, mottled underparts. Flight consists of fast wing beats alternating with circular glides. Purple Martins commonly use man-made nest boxes or tree hollows as nesting sites. (Illustration shows an adult male.)

Tree Swallow,
Tachycineta bicolor
Family Hirundinidae (Swallows)
Size: 5.75"
Season: Winter on the Coastal Plains,
summer in western mountains
Habitat: Variety of habitat near water
and perching sites

The Tree Swallow has a short, slightly notched tail; broad-based, triangular wings; and a thick neck. It has a high-contrast plumage pattern with dark metallic green-blue upperparts and crisp white underparts. In the perched bird, the primaries reach just past the tail tip. Juveniles show gray-brown below, with a subtle, darker breast band. Tree Swallows take insects on the wing but will also eat berries and fruits. The voice is a high-pitched chirping. The swallows often form huge lines of individuals perched on wires or branches. (Illustration shows an adult male.)

Northern Rough-winged Swallow,
Stelgidopteryx serripennis
Family Hirundinidae (Swallows)
Size: 5.5"
Season: Summer
Habitat: Sandy cliffs, steep
streamsides, outcrops, bridges

The Northern Rough-winged Swallow flies in a smooth and even fashion, with full wing beats, feeding on insects caught on the wing. It is uniform brownish above and white below. The breast is lightly streaked with pale brown, and the tail is short and square. Juveniles show light, rust-colored wing bars on the upper coverts. These fairly solitary swallows find nesting sites in holes in sandy cliffs. (Illustration shows an adult.)

Barn Swallow,
Hirundo rustica
Family Hirundinidae
(Swallows)
Size: 6.5"
Season: Summer
Habitat: Open rural areas
near bridges, old buildings, caves

The widespread and common Barn Swallow has narrow, pointed wings and a long, deeply forked tail. It is pale orange-brown (in males) or cream (in females) below and dark blue above, with a rusty orange forehead and throat. Barn Swallows are graceful, fluid fliers, and they often forage in groups to catch insects in flight. The voice is a loud, repetitive chirping or clicking. The swallows build a cup-shaped nest of mud on almost any protected man-made structure. (Illustration shows an adult male.)

Carolina Chickadee,
Poecile carolinensis
Family Paridae (Chickadees, Titmice)
Size: 4.75"
Season: Year-round
Habitat: Woodlands, rural gardens

The Carolina Chickadee is a small, compact, active bird with short, rounded wings. It is gray above and lighter gray or buff below, with a contrasting black cap and throat patch. It is quite similar to the Black-capped Chickadee, which occurs in more mountainous habitats. Its voice sounds like the name—*Chick-A-Dee-Dee-Dee*—or is a soft *Fee-Bay*. It is quite social and feeds on a variety of seeds, berries, and insects found in trees and shrubs. (Illustration shows an adult.)

Tufted Titmouse,
Baeolophus bicolor
Family Paridae
(Chickadees, Titmice)
Size: 6.5"
Season: Year-round
Habitat: Woodlands, urban areas

The tame and curious Tufted Titmouse is a small, chunky bird with short, broad wings and a conspicuous tuft on the crest. It is gray above and pale gray below, with a wash of orange along the sides and flanks. It has a small but sturdy black bill, large black eyes, and a black forehead. Titmice often form foraging groups with other species that flit through the vegetation picking out nuts, seeds, insects, and berries from the bark and twigs. At feeders Tufted Titmice prefer sunflower seeds. The voice is a repetitive *Peeta Peeta*. (Illustration shows an adult.)

White-breasted Nuthatch,
Sitta carolinensis
Family Sittidae (Nuthatches)
Size: 5.75"
Season: Year-round
Habitat: Mixed oak or coniferous woodlands

The White-breasted Nuthatch has a large head and wide neck; short, rounded wings; and a short tail. It is blue-gray above and pale gray below, with rusty smudging on the lower flanks and undertail coverts. The breast and face are white, and there is a black crown merging with the mantle. The bill is long, thin, and upturned at the tip. To forage it creeps headfirst down tree trunks to pick out insects and seeds. Its voice is a nasal, repetitive *Auk, auk, auk*. It nests in tree cavities high off the ground. (Illustration shows an adult male.)

Red-breasted Nuthatch,

Sitta canadensis
Family Sittidae (Nuthatches)
Size: 4.5"
Season: Winter
Habitat: Open coniferous and oak forests

The Red-breasted Nuthatch is a small, stubby bird with a large head, a short tail, and a long, thin, slightly upturned bill. Plumage is blue-gray above and rusty orange or buff (in the female) below. The head is white, with a black crown and eye stripe. The legs are short, but the toes are very long to aid in grasping tree bark. Nuthatches creep headfirst down tree trunks and branches to pick out insects and seeds. The call is a nasal, repetitive *Yonk, yonk, yonk*. (Illustration shows an adult male.)

Brown-headed Nuthatch,

Sitta pusilla
Family Sittidae (Nuthatches)
Size: 4.5"
Season: Year-round
Habitat: Pine woodlands

Clinging to tree trunks facing downward, the little Brown-headed Nuthatch creeps its way down the tree picking out insects, insect larvae, or seeds from the bark. It is a compact, short-necked, large-headed bird with a short, stubby tail. Its legs are short, but the toes are long to help the bird grasp bark. The bill is long, thin, sharp, and upturned at the tip. Plumage is gray above and lighter gray or buff-colored below. The head has a brown cap, a dark eye line, and a small white spot on the back of the nape. Brown-headed Nuthatches have undulating flight and build nests in cavities in tree trunks. (Illustration shows an adult.)

Brown Creeper,
Certhia americana
Family Certhiidae
(Creepers)
Size: 5.25"
Season: Winter
Habitat: Mature woodlands

The Brown Creeper is a small, cryptically colored bird with a long, pointed tail and a long, downcurved bill. It is mottled black, brown, and white above and plain white below, fading to brownish toward the rear. The face has a pale supercilium and a white chin. The legs are short, with long, grasping toes. Like a woodpecker's tail, the creeper's stiff tail helps support the bird. Brown Creepers spiral upward on tree trunks, probing for insects in the bark, then fly to the bottom of another tree to repeat the process. The voice is composed of thin, high-pitched *Seet* notes. (Illustration shows an adult.)

Carolina Wren,
Thryothorus ludovicianus
Family Troglodytidae (Wrens)
Size: 5.5"
Season: Year-round
Habitat: Understory of wooded
and brushy areas, swamps

The state bird of South Carolina, the Carolina Wren is a vocal but cryptic bird, usually hidden among dense foliage close to the ground. It lurks in vegetation, picking out insects, seeds, or fruit, and emitting a musical song or a harsh, quick call. The body is plump with a short, rounded tail and a thin, slightly downcurved bill. It is dark rusty brown above and buff-colored below and has a long, white superciliary stripe extending to the nape. The wings and tail are thinly barred with black. This Carolina Wren habitually holds its tail in a cocked-up position. (Illustration shows an adult.)

Winter Wren,
Troglodytes hiemalis
Family Troglodytidae (Wrens)
Size: 4"
Season: Winter
Habitat: Moist woodlands,
streamsides

The Winter Wren is a tiny, plump, short-tailed wren that is brown overall with dark mottling and barring. It is a bit paler on the throat and breast and has a distinct pale supercilium. The tail is commonly held cocked up, and the bill is held slightly tilted up. It forages through dense vegetation searching for insects. Inquisitive and curious, Winter Wrens may be lured into view by imitating their high-pitched, buzzy calls. (Illustration shows an adult.)

House Wren,
Troglodytes aedon
Family Troglodytidae (Wrens)
Size: 4.75"
Season: Year-round in the western uplands, winter elsewhere
Habitat: Shrubby areas, rural gardens

The House Wren is a loud, drab wren with short, rounded wings and a thin, pointed, downcurved bill. Plumage is brown and barred above and pale gray-brown beneath, with barring on the lower belly, undertail coverts, and tail. The head is lighter on the throat, at the lores, and above the eyes. House Wrens feed in the brush for insects and sing rapid, melodic, chirping songs, often while cocking their tails downward. (Illustration shows an adult.)

Marsh Wren,
Cistothorus palustris
Family Troglodytidae (Wrens)
Size: 5"
Season: Year-round along
the coast, winter inland
Habitat: Marshes, reeds, stream banks

The Marsh Wren is a small, cryptic, rufous-brown wren with a normally cocked-up tail. The tail and wings are barred with black, and the chin and breast are white. There is a well-defined white superciliary stripe below a uniform brown crown, and the mantle shows distinct black-and-white striping. The bill is long and slightly decurved. Marsh Wrens are vocal day and night, voicing quick, repetitive cheeping. They are secretive but inquisitive and glean insects from the marsh vegetation and water's surface. (Illustration shows an adult.)

Blue-gray Gnatcatcher,
Polioptila caerulea
Family Polioptilidae (Gnatcatchers)
Size: 4.5"
Season: Year-round
Habitat: Deciduous or
pine woodlands, thickets

The Blue-gray Gnatcatcher is a tiny, energetic, long-tailed bird with a narrow, pointed bill and thin, dark legs. It is blue-gray above and pale gray below, with white edges to the tertials creating a light patch on the middle of the folded wing. The tail is rounded and has black inner and white outer feathers. The eyes are surrounded by crisp, white eye rings. Males are brighter blue overall and have a darker supraloral line. To forage, gnatcatchers flit through thickets and catch insects in the air. They will often twitch and fan their tails. The voice is a high-pitched buzzing or cheeping sound, which sometimes sounds like the call of other birds. (Illustration shows an adult male.)

Golden-crowned Kinglet,
Regulus satrapa
Family Regulidae (Kinglets)
Size: 4"
Season: Winter
Habitat: Mixed woodlands, brushy areas

The Golden-crowned Kinglet is a tiny, plump songbird with a short tail and a short, pointed bill. It is greenish gray above, with wings patterned in black, white, and green, and is pale gray below. The face has a dark eye stripe and crown; the center of the crown is golden yellow and sometimes raised. The legs are dark with orange toes. Kinglets are in constant motion, flitting and dangling among branches, sometimes hanging upside down or hovering at the edge of branches to feed. The voice includes very high-pitched *Tzee* notes. (Illustration shows an adult.)

Ruby-crowned Kinglet,
Regulus calendula
Family Regulidae (Kinglets)
Size: 4"
Season: Winter
Habitat: Mixed woodlands, brushy areas

The Ruby-crowned Kinglet is a tiny, plump songbird with a short tail and a thin, diminutive bill. It has a habit of nervously twitching its wings as it actively flits through vegetation, gleaning small insects and larvae. It may also hover in search of food. Plumage is pale olive green above and paler below, with patterned wings and pale wing bars on the upper coverts. There are white eye rings or crescents around the eyes. The bright red crest of the male is only faintly noticeable unless the crest is raised. The voice is a very high-pitched, whistling *Seeee*. (Illustration shows an adult.)

Eastern Bluebird,
Sialia sialis
Family Turdidae
(Thrushes)
Size: 7"
Season: Year-round
Habitat: Open woodland,
pastures, fields

The Eastern Bluebird is a member of the thrush family that travels in small groups, feeding on a variety of insects, spiders, and berries and singing a series of musical *Chur-Lee* notes. It is a stocky, short-tailed and short-billed bird that often perches in an upright posture on wires and posts. The male is brilliant blue above and rusty orange below, with a white belly and undertail region. The orange extends to the nape, making a subtle collar. The female is paler overall, with a white throat and eye ring. Juveniles are brownish gray, with extensive white spotting and barred underparts. Man-made nest boxes have helped this species increase in numbers throughout its range. (Illustration shows an adult male, below, and a female, above.)

Hermit Thrush,
Catharus guttatus
Family Turdidae (Thrushes)
Size: 7"
Season: Winter
Habitat: Woodlands, brushy areas

The Hermit Thrush is a compact, short-tailed thrush that habitually cocks its tail. It forages on the ground near vegetative cover for insects, worms, and berries and voices a song of beautiful, flute-like notes. It is reddish to olive-brown above, with a rufous tail. Its underparts are white, with dusky flanks and sides and black spotting on the throat and breast. The dark eyes are encircled by white eye rings. In flight the pale wing lining contrasts with the dark flight feathers. (Illustration shows an adult.)

Wood Thrush,
Hylocichla mustelina
Family Turdidae (Thrushes)
Size: 7.75"
Season: Summer
Habitat: Dense, mixed woodlands;
suburban areas

The Wood Thrush is a solitary, fairly plump thrush with a short tail and a relatively large bill. It is rich reddish orange on the head, fading to a duller brown across the back and tail. Below, it is white with extensive dark spotting from the throat down to the flanks. There is a distinct white eye ring and a black-and-white-streaked auricular patch. The legs are thin and pale pink. The sexes are similar. Wood Thrushes hop through the undergrowth and along the ground for insects, worms, or berries and voice a beautiful, fluting song preceded by short, soft notes. (Illustration shows an adult.)

American Robin,
Turdus migratorius
Family Turdidae (Thrushes)
Size: 10"
Season: Year-round
Habitat: Widespread in a variety of habitats; woodlands, fields, parks, lawns

Familiar and friendly, the American Robin is a large thrush with a long tail and legs. It commonly holds its head cocked and wing tips lowered beneath its tail. It is gray-brown above and rufous below, with a darker head and contrasting white eye crescents and loral patches. The chin is streaked black and white, and the bill is yellow mixed with darker edges. Females are typically paler overall, and juveniles show spots of white above and dark spots below. Robins forage on the ground, picking out earthworms and insects, or in trees for berries. The robin's song is a series of high, musical phrases sounding like *Cheery, Cheer-U-Up, Cheerio*. (Illustration shows an adult male.)

Gray Catbird,
Dumetella carolinensis
Family Mimidae
(Mockingbirds, Catbirds, Thrashers)
Size: 8.5"
Season: Year-round
Habitat: Understory of woodland
edges, shrubs, rural gardens

The solitary Gray Catbird is long-necked and sleek, with a sturdy, pointed bill. It is uniformly gray except for its rufous undertail coverts, black crown, and black, rounded tail. It is quite secretive and spends most of its time hidden in thickets close to the ground, picking through the substrate for insects, berries, and seeds. Its call includes a nasal, catlike *Meew,* from which its name is derived, although it will also mimic the songs of other birds. To escape danger it will often choose to run away rather than fly. (Illustration shows an adult.)

Northern Mockingbird,
Mimus polyglottos
Family Mimidae
(Mockingbirds, Catbirds, Thrashers)
Size: 10.5"
Season: Year-round
Habitat: Open fields, grassy areas near
vegetative cover, suburbs, parks

The Northern Mockingbird is constantly vocalizing. Its scientific name, *polyglottos,* means "many voices," alluding to its amazing mimicry of the songs of other birds. It is sleek, long-tailed, and long-legged. Plumage is gray above, with darker wings and tail, and off-white to brownish gray below. There are two white wing bars; short, dark eye stripes; and pale eye rings. In flight conspicuous white patches on the inner primaries and coverts and white outer tail feathers can be seen. Like other mimids, mockingbirds forage on the ground for insects and berries, intermittently flicking their wings. (Illustration shows an adult.)

Brown Thrasher,
Toxostoma rufum
Family Mimidae
(Mockingbirds, Catbirds, Thrashers)
Size: 11"
Season: Year-round
Habitat: Woodlands, thickets,
urban gardens, orchards

The Brown Thrasher is primarily a ground-dwelling bird that thrashes through leaves and dirt for insects and plant material. It has a long tail and long legs and a medium-length, slightly decurved bill. Plumage is rufous brown above, including the tail, and whitish below, heavily streaked with brown or black. There are two prominent, pale wing bars, and the outermost corners of the tail are pale. The eyes are yellow to orange. The thrasher's voice includes a variety of musical phrases, often sung from a conspicuous perch. (Illustration shows an adult.)

European Starling,
Sturnus vulgaris
Family Sturnidae (Starlings)
Size: 8.5"
Season: Year-round
Habitat: Found almost anywhere,
particularly rural fields, gardens, dumps,
urban parks

Introduced from Europe, the European Starling has successfully infiltrated most habitats in North America and competes with native birds for nest cavities. It is a stocky, sturdy, aggressive bird that is glossy black overall, with a green or purple sheen. The breeding adult has a yellow bill and greater iridescence; the winter adult is more flat black, with a black bill and numerous white spots. The tail is short and square. Starlings form very large, compact flocks and fly directly on pointed, triangular wings. The diet of starlings is highly variable and includes insects, grains, and berries. Vocalizations include loud, wheezy whistles and clucks and imitations of other birdsongs. (Illustration shows a breeding adult.)

STARLINGS

Cedar Waxwing,
Bombycilla cedrorum
Family Bombycillidae (Waxwings)
Size: 7"
Season: Year-round in western mountains, winter elsewhere in South Carolina
Habitat: Woodlands, swamps, urban areas near berry trees

The Cedar Waxwing is a compact, crested songbird with pointed wings and a short tail. Plumage is sleek and smooth, brownish gray overall with paler underparts, a yellowish wash on the belly, and white undertail coverts. The head pattern is striking, with a crisp black mask thinly bordered by white. The tail is tipped with bright yellow. Tips of the secondary feathers are a unique, red waxy substance. Cedar Waxwings form large flocks and devour berries from one tree, then move on to the next. They may also flycatch small insects. The waxwing's voice is an extremely high-pitched, whistling *Seee*. (Illustration shows an adult.)

Golden-winged Warbler,
Vermivora chrysoptera
Family Parulidae (Wood-Warblers)
Size: 4.75"
Season: Summer
Habitat: Woodland edges, brushy fields

The Golden-winged Warbler has a long, thin, sharp bill that it uses to extract and pick insects and larvae. Plumage is gray above and pale gray or whitish below, and the tail has white outer corners. Yellow wing coverts create a broad yellow patch on the upper wings. Males have a striking black facial mask and throat and a yellow forecrown. Females are similarly patterned but with a gray mask and throat and a duller yellow crown. Golden-winged Warblers build nests in thickets on the ground. (Illustration shows a breeding male, below, and a female, above.)

Northern Parula,
Parula americana
Family Parulidae (Wood-Warblers)
Size: 4.5"
Season: Summer
Habitat: Woodland treetops

The Northern Parula is a tiny, stubby warbler with a short, sharp bill, a short tail, and a relatively large head. The upperparts are slate blue with a greenish mantle. Below, there is a white belly and undertail, a yellow chin and breast, and a rufous breast band. There are white eye arcs above and below the eyes, and the lower mandible is yellow. The wing shows two bold, white wing bars. The female is bordered above the breast band with gray. Northern Parulas forage for insects and caterpillars in trees. (Illustration shows an adult male.)

Yellow-rumped Warbler (Myrtle Warbler),
Dendroica coronata coronata
Family Parulidae (Wood-Warblers)
Size: 5.5"
Season: Winter
Habitat: Deciduous and coniferous woodlands, suburbs

Two races of this species occur in North America. The "myrtle" form is dispersed across North America, and the "Audubon's" form is seen west of the Rockies. The Myrtle Warbler is blue-gray above with dark streaks and is white below, with black streaking below the chin and a bright yellow side patch. There is a black mask across the face bordered by a thin superciliary stripe above and a white throat below. The nonbreeding adult and the female are paler, with a more brownish cast to the upperparts. The longish tail has white spots on both sides and meets with the conspicuous yellow rump. These warblers prefer to eat myrtle berries and insects. (Illustration shows a breeding male in "myrtle" form.)

Yellow-throated Warbler,
Dendroica dominica
Family Parulidae (Wood-Warblers)
Size: 5.25"
Season: Summer
Habitat: Coniferous and mixed
woodlands near water

The Yellow-throated Warbler is an elongated, long-billed warbler that forages high in the tree canopy, picking insects from bark. Plumage is slate gray above and white below, heavily streaked with black, and the chin and breast are a clean yellow. There is a bold face pattern with a white supercilium and lower eye arc bordered by a black eye stripe and auricular area. Behind the ear is a distinctive white patch. The dark back contrasts with two white wing bars, and the outer tail feathers show patches of white. (Illustration shows an adult male.)

Pine Warbler, *Dendroica pinus*
Family Parulidae (Wood-Warblers)
Size: 5.5"
Season: Year-round
Habitat: Pine and mixed pine woodlands

The Pine Warbler creeps along pine branches picking insects from the bark. It is a rounded, long-winged warbler with a relatively thick bill. Plumage is olive green above with gray wings, and yellow below streaked with olive. Belly and undertail coverts are white. The yellow of the chin extends under the auricular area; faint "spectacles" are formed by the light lores and eye rings, and there are two clearly marked white wing bars. The female is paler overall, and juveniles lack yellow on the chin and underparts. The outer tail feathers show white patches. (Illustration shows an adult male.)

Prairie Warbler,
Dendroica discolor
Family Parulidae (Wood-Warblers)
Size: 4.5"
Season: Summer
Habitat: Mangroves,
early succession forests, shrubs

The Prairie Warbler is a small, plump, long-tailed warbler with a rising, buzzy song, sometimes sung from a treetop perch. It is olive green above and bright yellow below, with black streaking along the sides topped by a distinct spot just behind the bottom of the chin. A dark half-circle swoops underneath the eye, and rusty streaking is sometimes seen on the mantle. The female is slightly paler overall. The outer tail feathers are white. Prairie Warblers forage through low branches of the understory for insects and spiders. (Illustration shows an adult male.)

Black-and-white Warbler,
Mniotilta varia
Family Parulidae (Wood-Warblers)
Size: 5.25"
Season: Summer
Habitat: Mixed woodlands

WOOD-WARBLERS

The Black-and-white Warbler is a unique warbler that behaves more like a nuthatch, creeping up and down tree trunks probing for insects in the bark with its long, downcurved bill. The breeding male is streaked black and white overall and has a black throat, auricular patch, and crown. The crown is topped with a thin white medial stripe. Females have paler streaking on the undersides, a white throat, gray auriculars, and buff-colored flanks. Both sexes have black spotting on the undertail coverts. The voice is a series of high-pitched *See-See-See* notes or a quick *Seeta-Seeta-Seeta*. (Illustration shows a breeding male, below, and a female, above.)

American Redstart,

Setophaga ruticilla
Family Parulidae
(Wood-Warblers)
Size: 5"
Season: Summer
Habitat: Open mixed woodlands
in early succession

The constantly active, frenetic American Redstart often fans its tail and wings in display while perched. It is long-tailed, and the plumages of males and females are markedly different. The male is jet black above and white below, with a fiery red patch at the side of the breast and a paler, peachy red in a wing bar and on the sides of its tail. The female is gray-green above, with a slate gray head and a white chin and breast. The colored areas are located on the same parts as on the male but are yellow. Redstarts eat insects gleaned from branches and bark or flycatch for insects. (Illustration shows an adult male, below, and a female, above.)

Prothonotary Warbler,

Protonotaria citrea
Family Parulidae
(Wood-Warblers)
Size: 5.5"
Season: Summer
Habitat: Wooded swamps

Also known as the Golden Swamp Warbler, the Prothonotary Warbler is a fairly large warbler with a short tail, a relatively large head, and a long, sharp bill. The head and underparts are a rich yellow to yellow-orange; the undertail coverts are white. The wings and tail are blue-gray, and there is an olive green mantle. Females and juveniles are paler overall, with an olive cast to the head. Prothonotary Warblers forage through the understory for insects. (Illustration shows an adult male.)

Worm-eating Warbler,
Helmitheros vermivorum
Family Parulidae (Wood-Warblers)
Size: 5.25"
Season: Summer
Habitat: Dense growth in woodlands, often near streams

The Worm-eating Warbler is a plain-looking, relatively large warbler with a short, stubby tail and a thick, long bill. The sexes have similar plumage: olive-brown above and pale buff below, with no apparent wing bars or tail spots. The only obvious markings are on the head, which has two thin black crown stripes and thin black eye lines. The legs are pale pinkish or flesh-colored. Worm-eating Warblers forage on or close to the ground for insects and larvae, not necessarily just worms, as the common name would imply. Their song is a rapid trill of dry, toneless, buzzy notes. (Illustration shows an adult.)

Louisiana Waterthrush,
Parkesia motacilla
Family Parulidae
(Wood-Warblers)
Size: 6"
Season: Summer
Habitat: Wooded areas near streamsides

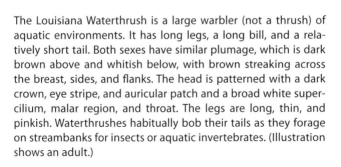

The Louisiana Waterthrush is a large warbler (not a thrush) of aquatic environments. It has long legs, a long bill, and a relatively short tail. Both sexes have similar plumage, which is dark brown above and whitish below, with brown streaking across the breast, sides, and flanks. The head is patterned with a dark crown, eye stripe, and auricular patch and a broad white supercilium, malar region, and throat. The legs are long, thin, and pinkish. Waterthrushes habitually bob their tails as they forage on streambanks for insects or aquatic invertebrates. (Illustration shows an adult.)

Common Yellowthroat,
Geothlypis trichas
Family Parulidae
(Wood-Warblers)
Size: 5"
Season: Year-round
Habitat: Low vegetation near water,
swamps, fields

The Common Yellowthroat scampers through the undergrowth looking for insects and spiders in a somewhat wrenlike manner. It is a plump little warbler that often cocks up its tail. Plumage is olive-brown above and pale brown to whitish below, with a bright yellow breast/chin region and undertail coverts. The male has a black facial mask trailed by a fuzzy white area on the nape. Females lack the facial mask. (Illustration shows an adult male, below, and a female, above.)

Hooded Warbler,
Wilsonia citrina
Family Parulidae
(Wood-Warblers)
Size: 5"
Season: Summer
Habitat: Moist woodlands, swamps

The Hooded Warbler lurks in the woodland understory, picking out insects while continually flicking its tail and singing its high, musical *Weeta-Weeta-Weeta-Toe*. Plumage is olive green above and bright yellow below. The male has a full black hood encompassing the face and chin; the female has a fainter, partial mask and a yellow chin. White inner vanes to the outer tail feathers can be seen in the fanned tail. (Illustration shows an adult male, below, and a female, above.)

Yellow-breasted Chat,

Icteria virens
Family Parulidae (Wood-Warblers)
Size: 7.5"
Season: Summer
Habitat: Dense vegetation,
woodland edges

The largest wood-warbler, the Yellow-breasted Chat has a long, rounded tail and a heavy, black, pointed bill with a strongly curved culmen. It is uniformly greenish brown above. Below, the belly and undertail coverts are white, while the chin and breast are bright yellow. The head is dark, with bold white patterning above the lores, at the malar area, and around the eyes, forming white "spectacles." Females are slightly duller in color. Yellow-breasted Chats forage in low brush for insects and berries and have quite variable vocalizations, including mimicking the songs of other birds. The male has a strange display behavior in which he hovers and dangles his legs. (Illustration shows an adult.)

Eastern Towhee,

Pipilo erythrophthalmus
Family Emberizidae (Sparrows)
Size: 8"
Season: Year-round
Habitat: Thickets, suburban
shrubs, gardens

The Eastern Towhee is a large, long-tailed sparrow with a thick, short bill and sturdy legs. It forages on the ground in dense cover by kicking back both feet at once to uncover insects, seeds, and worms. It is black above, including the head and upper breast, and has rufous sides and a white belly. The base of the primaries and the corners of the tail are white. Eye color ranges from red to white, depending on the region. Females are similar to the males but are brown above. The towhee's song is a musical *Drink-Your-Teee*. The Eastern Towhee was once conspecific with the Spotted Towhee as the Rufous-sided Towhee. (Illustration shows an adult male.)

Bachman's Sparrow,

Peucaea aestivalis
Family Emberizidae (Sparrows)
Size: 6"
Season: Year-round
Habitat: Scrub or grass
in open pine woodlands

The Bachman's Sparrow is named for a Charleston minister who was a friend of John James Audubon . It is large and chunky, with a thick, relatively long bill for a sparrow. The sexes are similar, with upperparts that are streaked gray, brown, and black; the underparts are pale buff with a white belly and no streaking. The head is buff-gray with a reddish lateral crown stripe and eye lines. The legs are pale pink. The somewhat rounded tail can be seen in flight. Bachman's Sparrows stay close to the ground or may vocalize from a conspicuous perch with a song consisting of a rapid series of monotone chip or *Tseet* notes. (Illustration shows an adult.)

Chipping Sparrow,

Spizella passerina
Family Emberizidae (Sparrows)
Size: 5.5"
Season: Year-round
Habitat: Dry fields, woodland edges, gardens

The Chipping Sparrow is a medium-size sparrow with a slightly notched tail and a rounded crest. It is barred black and brown on the upperparts, has a gray rump, and is pale gray below. The head has a rufous crown, white superciliary stripes, dark eye lines, and a white throat. The bill is short, conical, and pointed. Sexes are similar. Winter adults are duller and lack rufous on the crown. Chipping Sparrows feed from trees or open ground in loose flocks, searching for seeds and insects. The voice is a rapid, staccato chipping sound. (Illustration shows a breeding adult.)

Field Sparrow,
Spizella pusilla
Family Emberizidae (Sparrows)
Size: 5.75"
Season: Year-round
Habitat: Fields with bushy cover or scattered trees

The Field Sparrow is a rather slender sparrow with a long, notched tail and a thick-based, pinkish bill. It is brownish above, with dark streaking and pale wing bars, and grayish below, with a rufous wash along the breast and flanks. The head is mostly gray, with a rufous crown and upper auricular patches and distinct, thin white eye rings. The sexes are similar. Juveniles are duller overall, with moderate dark streaking on the breast. Field Sparrows forage on the ground and in brush for seeds and insects. The song, often vocalized from a conspicuous perch, is a series of clear, high notes that gradually increase in speed. (Illustration shows an adult.)

Grasshopper Sparrow,
Ammodramus savannarum
Family Emberizidae (Sparrows)
Size: 5"
Season: Year-round
Habitat: Grassland with scrub

The Grasshopper Sparrow has a large, flattened head and a short tail. It is streaked brown, white, and black above and unstreaked buff below. The head is plain buff, with a darkish spot on the cheek and a light medial stripe between dark crown stripes. The sexes are similar. Juveniles show noticeable streaking across the breast and flanks. Grasshopper Sparrows feed in grasses or on the ground for grasshoppers (of course!), other insects, and seeds. The voice is a thin, drawn out buzzy song and short *Chip* notes, sometimes sung from a conspicuous perch. The sparrows often run when alarmed or fly in erratic, weak spurts. (Illustration shows an adult.)

Seaside Sparrow,
Ammodramus maritimus
Family Emberizidae (Sparrows)
Size: 6″
Season: Year-round
Habitat: Coastal saltwater marshes, freshwater marshes

The Seaside Sparrow is plump with a relatively large, flat head, a fairly long bill, and a short tail. Plumage is olive-brown above, with dark streaking; underparts are white, with dark streaks or spots. The white chin is bordered by an obvious moustachial stripe, and the supraloral region is yellow. Seaside sparrows forage among the marsh vegetation for insects, seeds, and small crustaceans and snails, diving quickly into cover from flight. (Illustration shows an adult.)

Song Sparrow,
Melospiza melodia
Family Emberizidae (Sparrows)
Size: 6″
Season: Winter
Habitat: Thickets, shrubs, woodland edges near water

One of the most common sparrows, the Song Sparrow is fairly plump, with a long, rounded tail. It is brown and gray with streaking above and white below, with heavy dark streaking that often converges at a discrete spot in the middle of the breast. The head has a dark crown with a gray medial stripe, dark eye lines, and a dark malar stripe above the white chin. Song sparrows are usually seen in small groups or individually foraging on the ground for insects and seeds. The song consists of a few clear, deliberate notes followed by a rapid trill; the call is a *Chip, chip, chip.* (Illustration shows an adult.)

White-throated Sparrow,
Zonotrichia albicollis
Family Emberizidae (Sparrows)
Size: 6.5"
Season: Winter
Habitat: Undergrowth of mixed woodlands, thickets, gardens

The White-throated Sparrow is a fairly large, round sparrow with a long tail and a typically short, thick bill. It is brown with dark streaking above, has a gray rump, and is grayish below, washed with brown and lightly streaked. The head has a black crown that is bisected by a white medial strip, white superciliary stripes with yellow near the lores, and dark eye lines. The white chin is sharply bordered by the gray breast below. White-throated Sparrows forage on the ground in small flocks, often with other species, picking up insects and seeds. The sparrow's song is a clean, piercing, simple whistle that mimics the phrase *Old Sam Peabody, Peabody, Peabody.* (Illustration shows an adult.)

Summer Tanager,
Piranga rubra
Family Cardinalidae
(Cardinals, Tanagers, Grosbeaks, Buntings)
Size: 7.75"
Season: Summer
Habitat: Mixed pine and oak woodlands

The Summer Tanager lives high in the tree canopy, where it voices a musical song and forages for insects and fruit. It is a relatively large, heavy-billed tanager with a crown that is often peaked in the middle. The male has variable shades of red over the entire body; the female is olive or brownish yellow above and dull yellow below. Juveniles are similar to the females but have a patchy red head and breast. (Illustration shows an adult male.)

Northern Cardinal,
Cardinalis cardinalis
Family Cardinalidae
(Cardinals, Tanagers, Grosbeaks, Buntings)
Size: 8.5"
Season: Year-round
Habitat: Woodlands with thickets,
suburban gardens

The Northern Cardinal, with its thick, powerful bill, eats mostly seeds but will also forage for fruit and insects. Often found in pairs, cardinals are quite common at suburban feeders. This long-tailed songbird has a thick, short, orange bill and a tall crest. The male is red overall, with a black mask and chin. The female is brownish above and dusky below, crested, and has a dark front to the face. Juveniles are similar to the females but have a black bill. The cardinal's voice is a musical *Weeta-Weeta* or *Woit,* heard from a tall, exposed perch. (Illustration shows an adult male, below, and a female, above.)

Blue Grosbeak, *Guiraca caerulea*
Family Cardinalidae (Cardinals, Tanagers,
Grosbeaks, Buntings)
Size: 6.5"
Season: Summer
Habitat: Woodland edges, thickets,
fields

The name "grosbeak" derives from the French word *gros,* meaning "large," and refers to their massive, conical bills. The male Blue Grosbeak is azure blue overall, with rufous wing bars and shoulder patches, black at the front of the face, and a horn-colored bill. The female is brown overall and paler below, with lighter wing bars and lores. The similar Indigo Bunting is smaller, has a smaller bill, and lacks the rufous color on the wings. Blue Grosbeaks eat seeds, fruit, and insects in open areas and habitually flick their tails. They often perch and sing a meandering, warbling song for extended periods. (Illustration shows an adult male, below, and a female, above.)

Indigo Bunting,

Passerina cyanea
Family Cardinalidae
(Cardinals, Tanagers, Grosbeaks, Buntings)
Size: 5.5"
Season: Summer
Habitat: Brush, open woodlands, fields

Often occurring in large flocks, the Indigo Bunting forages mostly on the ground for insects, berries, and seeds. It is a small, compact songbird with a short, thick bill. The male is entirely blue, the head being a dark, purplish blue and the body a lighter, sky blue. The female is brownish gray above and duller below, with faint streaking on the breast meeting a white throat. The winter male is smudged with patchy gray, brown, and white. Buntings perch in treetops, voicing their undulating, chirping melodies. (Illustration shows a breeding male, below, and a female, above.)

Red-winged Blackbird,

Agelaius phoeniceus
Family Icteridae
(Blackbirds, Grackles, Orioles)
Size: 8.5"
Season: Year-round
Habitat: Marshes, meadows, agricultural areas near water

The Red-winged Blackbird is a widespread, ubiquitous, chunky meadow-dweller that forms huge flocks during the nonbreeding season. The male is deep black overall, with bright orange-red lesser coverts and pale median coverts that form an obvious shoulder patch in flight but may be partially concealed on the perched bird. The female is barred tan and dark brown overall, with pale superciliary stripes and a pale malar patch. The blackbirds forage the marshland for insects, spiders, and seeds. The voice is a loud, raspy, vibrating *Konk-A-Leee,* delivered from a perch atop a tall reed or branch. (Illustration shows an adult male, below, and a female, above.)

Eastern Meadowlark,

Sturnella magna
Family Icteridae
(Blackbirds, Grackles, Orioles)
Size: 9.5"
Season: Year-round
Habitat: Open fields, grasslands, meadows

The Eastern Meadowlark is a chunky, short-tailed icterid with a flat head and a long, pointed bill. It is heavily streaked and barred above and yellow beneath, with dark streaking. The head has a dark crown, white superciliary stripes, dark eye lines, and a yellow chin. On the upper breast is a black, V-shaped "necklace" that becomes quite pale during winter. Meadowlarks gather in loose flocks to pick through grasses for insects and seeds. They often perch on telephone wires or posts to sing their short, whistling phrases. (Illustration shows a breeding adult.)

Rusty Blackbird, *Euphagus carolinus*
Family Icteridae (Blackbirds, Grackles, Orioles)
Size: 9"
Season: Winter
Habitat: Marshes, riversides, pastures near water

The Rusty Blackbird is a sleek, medium-size blackbird that resembles the Brewer's Blackbird, whose range is farther west. The breeding male is matte black overall, with contrasting pale yellow eyes. The winter male is dark, barred with rusty brown along the back and breast, and has a mostly brown head except for the lores and auricular area. The winter female is paler still, with lighter brown above and on the head, and has a grayish rump. Rusty Blackbirds feed in small flocks in shallow water for aquatic invertebrates or in nearby fields for seeds. Their song is a series of chattery, squeaky, jumbled notes accented at the end with a louder, high-pitched *EE*. Once quite abundant, the Rusty Blackbird's numbers have decreased dramatically in recent years. (Illustration shows a breeding male, below, and a female, above.)

Common Grackle, *Quiscalus quiscula*
Family Icteridae (Blackbirds, Grackles, Orioles)
Size: 12.5"
Season: Year-round
Habitat: Pastures, open woodlands, urban parks

The Common Grackle is a large blackbird but is smaller than the Boat-tailed Grackle. The body is elongated, with a long, heavy bill and a long tail that is fatter toward the tip and is often folded into a keel shape. Plumage is black overall, with a metallic sheen of purple on the head and brown on the wings and underside. The eyes are a contrasting light yellow. Quite social, grackles form huge flocks with other blackbirds and forage on the ground for just about any kind of food, including insects, grains, crustaceans, even refuse. The voice is a high-pitched, rasping trill. (Illustration shows an adult male.)

Boat-tailed Grackle,
Quiscalus major
Family Icteridae
(Blackbirds, Grackles, Orioles)
Size: 14–16"; males larger than females
Season: Year-round
Habitat: Salt or freshwater marshes near the coast

The Boat-tailed Grackle is larger than the Common Grackle and is less likely to form large flocks. It has long legs and a long, broad, spatula-shaped tail that is often folded into a keel shape. The male is black overall, with a metallic blue-green sheen over the head and body. The female is smaller with a shorter tail, is brownish overall, and has a lighter head with dark striping along the eye lines, under the crown, and along the malar area. The eyes are light yellow, although individuals in southern Florida have darker, brown eyes. Grackles pick the ground for insects, seeds, and crustaceans. (Illustration shows an adult male, below, and a female, above.)

Brown-headed Cowbird,

Molothrus ater
Family Icteridae (Blackbirds, Grackles, Orioles)
Size: 7.5"
Season: Year-round
Habitat: Woodland edges, pastures
with livestock, grassy fields

The Brown-headed Cowbird is a stocky, short-winged, short-tailed blackbird with a short, conical bill. The male is glossy black overall, with a chocolate-brown head. The female is light brown overall, with faint streaking on the underparts and a pale throat. Cowbirds often feed in flocks with other blackbirds, picking seeds and insects from the ground. Vocalizations consist of a number of gurgling, squeaking phrases. Cowbirds practice brood parasitism, whereby they lay their eggs in the nests of other passerine species that then raise their young. Hence their presence often reduces the populations of other songbirds. (Illustration shows an adult male.)

Orchard Oriole, *Icterus spurius*

Family Icteridae
(Blackbirds, Grackles, Orioles)
Size: 7"
Season: Summer
Habitat: Orchards, open woodlands,
parks

The Orchard Oriole is a small oriole with a relatively thin, short bill and a short tail that it often tilts sideways. The male is black above, with a red rump and a black, hooded head. The underside is reddish or orange-brown with similarly colored shoulder patches. The lower mandible is light blue-gray. Females are markedly different, being greenish gray above and bright yellow below, with two white wing bars. Juveniles are similar to females but have a black chin and lores. Orchard Orioles feed in trees for insects, fruit, and nectar. They emit high, erratic, musical whistles and chirps. (Illustration shows an adult male, below, and a female, above.)

BLACKBIRDS, GRACKLES, ORIOLES

Baltimore Oriole, *Icterus galbula*
Family Icteridae (Blackbirds, Grackles, Orioles)
Size: 8.5"
Season: Winter along the coast, summer inland
Habitat: Deciduous woodlands, suburban gardens, parks

The Baltimore Oriole is a somewhat stocky icterid with a short, squared tail and a straight, tapered bill. The male is bright yellow-orange with a black hood. The wings are black, with white edging the flight feathers and coverts and yellow-orange shoulder patches. The tail is orange, with black along the base and down the middle. The female is paler along the sides, with white shoulder patches and a mottled yellow-and-brown head and plain tail. The oriole forages in the leafy canopy for insects, fruit, and nectar. The Baltimore Oriole is sometimes considered with Bullock's Oriole as one species, the Northern Oriole. (Illustration shows an adult male, below, and a female, above.)

House Finch, *Carpodacus mexicanus*
Family Fringillidae (Finches)
Size: 6"
Season: Year-round
Habitat: Woodland edges, urban areas

The House Finch is a western species that has been introduced to eastern North America and is now common and widespread across the country, especially in urban areas. It is a relatively slim finch with a longish, slightly notched tail and a short, conical bill with a downcurved culmen. The male is brown above, with streaking on the back, and pale below, with heavy streaking. An orange-red wash pervades the supercilium, throat, and upper breast. The female is a drab gray-brown, with similar streaking on the back and underside and no red on the face or breast. House Finches have a variable diet that includes seeds, insects, and fruit, and they are often the most abundant birds visiting feeders. The voice is a rapid, musical warble. (Illustration shows an adult male.)

American Goldfinch, *Spinus tristis*
Family Fringillidae (Finches)
Size: 5"
Season: Year-round in western uplands, winter elsewhere
Habitat: Open fields, marshes, urban feeders

The American Goldfinch is a small, cheerful, social finch with a short, notched tail and a small, conical bill. In winter it is brownish gray, lighter underneath, with black wings and tail. There is bright yellow on the shoulder, around the eyes, and along the chin, along with two white wing bars. In breeding plumage the male becomes light yellow across the back, undersides, and head and develops a black forehead and loral area. Also, the bill becomes orange. Females are similar to the males in winter plumage. Goldfinches forage by actively searching for insects and seeds of all kinds, particularly thistle seeds. The voice is a meandering, musical warble that includes high *Cheep* notes. (Illustration shows a breeding male, below, and a nonbreeding male, above.)

House Sparrow,
Passer domesticus
Family Passeridae (Old World Sparrows)
Size: 6.25"
Season: Year-round
Habitat: Urban environments, rural pastures

Introduced from Europe, the House Sparrow is ubiquitous in almost every city in the United States and is often the only sparrow-type bird seen in urban areas. It is stocky, aggressive, and gregarious and has a relatively large head and a short, finchlike bill. Males are streaked brown and black above and pale below. The lores, chin, and breast are black; the crown and auriculars are gray. In winter the male lacks the dark breast patch. Females are drab overall, with a lighter bill and pale supercilium. House Sparrows have a varied diet, including grains, insects, berries, and crumbs from the local cafe. The voice is a series of rather unmusical chirps. (Illustration shows a breeding male, below, and a female, above.)

Index

A

Acadian Flycatcher
(*Empidonax virescens*), 54
American Bittern (*Botaurus
lentiginosus*), 15
American Coot (*Fulica
americana*), 30
American Crow (*Corvus
brachyrhynchos*), 59
American Goldfinch (*Spinus
tristis*), 90
American Kestrel (*Falco
sparverius*), 26
American Oystercatcher
(*Haematopus palliatus*), 32
American Redstart (*Setophaga
ruticilla*), 76
American Robin (*Turdus
migratorius*), 69
American Widgeon (*Anas
americana*), 3
American Woodcock (*Scolopax
minor*), 37
Anhinga (*Anhinga anhinga*), 14

B

Bachman's Sparrow (*Peucaea
aestivalis*), 80
Bald Eagle (*Haliaeetus
leucocephalus*), 24
Baltimore Oriole (*Icterus
galbula*), 89
Barn Owl (*Tyto alba*), 45
Barn Swallow (*Hirundo
rustica*), 61
Barred Owl (*Strix varia*), 47
Belted Kingfisher (*Megaceryle
alcyon*), 49
Black-and-white Warbler
(*Mniotilta varia*), 75

Black-bellied Plover (*Pluvialis
squatarola*), 30
Black-crowned Night-Heron
(*Nycticorax nycticorax*), 19
Black-necked Stilt (*Himantopus
mexicanus*), 32
Black Rail (*Laterallus
jamaicensis*), 27
Black Skimmer (*Rynchops
niger*), 43
Black Vulture (*Coragyps
atratus*), 21
Blue-gray Gnatcatcher
(*Polioptila caerulea*), 66
Blue Grosbeak (*Guiraca
caerulea*), 84
Blue-headed Vireo (*Vireo
solitarius*), 57
Blue Jay (*Cyanocitta
cristata*), 58
Boat-tailed Grackle (*Quiscalus
major*), 87
Bonaparte's Gull
(*Chroicocephalus
philadelphia*), 38
Broad-winged Hawk (*Buteo
lineatus*), 25
Brown Creeper (*Certhia
americana*), 64
Brown-headed Cowbird
(*Molothrus ater*), 88
Brown-headed Nuthatch (*Sitta
pusilla*), 63
Brown Pelican (*Pelecanus
occidentalis*), 14
Brown Thrasher (*Toxostoma
rufum*), 71
Bufflehead (*Bucephala
albeola*), 7

C

Canada Goose *(Branta canadensis)*, 1
Carolina Chickadee *(Poecile carolinensis)*, 61
Carolina Wren *(Thryothorus ludovicianus)*, 64
Caspian Tern *(Sterna caspia)*, 42
Cattle Egret *(Bubulcus ibis)*, 18
Cedar Waxwing *(Bombycilla cedrorum)*, 72
Chimney Swift *(Chaetura pelagica)*, 48
Chipping Sparrow *(Spizella passerina)*, 80
Chuck-will's-widow *(Caprimulgus carolinensis)*, 48
Clapper Rail *(Rallus longirostris)*, 28
Common Goldeneye *(Bucephala clangula)*, 7
Common Grackle *(Quiscalus quiscula)*, 87
Common Loon *(Gavia immer)*, 11
Common Moorhen *(Gallinula chloropus)*, 29
Common Nighthawk *(Chordeiles minor)*, 47
Common Yellowthroat *(Geothlypis trichas)*, 78
Cooper's Hawk *(Accipiter cooperii)*, 24

D

Double-crested Cormorant *(Phalacrocorax auritus)*, 13
Downy Woodpecker *(Picoides pubescens)*, 51
Dunlin *(Calidris alpina)*, 37

E

Eastern Bluebird *(Sialia sialis)*, 68
Eastern Kingbird *(Tyrannus tyrannus)*, 55
Eastern Meadowlark *(Sturnella magna)*, 86
Eastern Phoebe *(Sayornis phoebe)*, 54
Eastern Screech-Owl *(Megascops asio)*, 46
Eastern Towhee *(Pipilo erythrophthalmus)*, 79
Eastern Wood-Pewee *(Contopus virens)*, 53
Eurasian Collared-Dove *(Streptopelia decaocto)*, 44
European Starling *(Sturnus vulgaris)*, 71

F

Field Sparrow *(Spizella pusilla)*, 81
Forster's Tern *(Sterna forsteri)*, 41

G

Gadwall *(Anas strepera)*, 2
Golden-crowned Kinglet *(Regulus satrapa)*, 67
Golden-winged Warbler *(Vermivora chrysoptera)*, 72
Grasshopper Sparrow *(Ammodramus savannarum)*, 81
Gray Catbird *(Dumetella carolinensis)*, 70
Great Black-backed Gull *(Larus marinus)*, 40
Great Blue Heron *(Ardea herodias)*, 16
Great Crested Flycatcher *(Myiarchus crinitus)*, 55

Great Egret *(Ardea alba)*, 16
Great Horned Owl *(Bubo virginianus)*, 46
Greater Yellowlegs *(Tringa melanoleuca)*, 33
Green Heron *(Butorides virescens)*, 19
Green-Winged Teal *(Anas crecca)*, 5

H

Hermit Thrush *(Catharus guttatus)*, 68
Herring Gull *(Larus argentatus)*, 39
Hooded Merganser *(Lophodytes cucullatus)*, 8
Hooded Warbler *(Wilsonia citrina)*, 78
Horned Grebe *(Podiceps auritus)*, 11
House Finch *(Carpodacus mexicanus)*, 89
House Sparrow *(Passer domesticus)*, 90
House Wren *(Troglodytes aedon)*, 65

I

Indigo Bunting *(Passerina cyanea)*, 85

K

Killdeer *(Charadrius vociferus)*, 31

L

Laughing Gull *(Leucophaeus atricilla)*, 38
Least Bittern *(Ixobrychus exilis)*, 15
Least Tern *(Sternula antillarum)*, 40

Lesser Scaup *(Aythya affinis)*, 6
Little Blue Heron *(Egretta caerulea)*, 17
Loggerhead Shrike *(Lanius ludovicianus)*, 56
Louisiana Waterthrush *(Parkesia motacilla)*, 77

M

Mallard *(Anas platyrhynchos)*, 3
Marbled Godwit *(Limosa fedoa)*, 34
Marsh Wren *(Cistothorus palustris)*, 66
Mississippi Kite *(Ictinia mississippiensis)*, 23
Mourning Dove *(Zenaida macroura)*, 44
Myrtle Warbler *(Dendroica coronata coronata)*, 73

N

Northern Bobwhite *(Colinus virginianus)*, 9
Northern Cardinal *(Cardinalis cardinalis)*, 84
Northern Flicker *(Colaptes auratus)*, 52
Northern Gannet *(Morus bassanus)*, 12
Northern Harrier *(Circus cyaneus)*, 23
Northern Mockingbird *(Mimus polyglottos)*, 70
Northern Parula *(Parula americana)*, 73
Northern Pintail *(Anas acuta)*, 4
Northern Rough-winged Swallow *(Stelgidopteryx serripennis)*, 60
Northern Shoveler *(Anas clypeata)*, 4

O

Orchard Oriole *(Icterus spurius)*, 88
Osprey *(Pandion haliaetus)*, 22

P

Peregrine Falcon *(Falco peregrinus)*, 27
Pied-billed Grebe *(Podilymbus podiceps)*, 12
Pileated Woodpecker *(Dryocopus pileatus)*, 52
Pine Warbler *(Dendroica pinus)*, 74
Prairie Warbler *(Dendroica discolor)*, 75
Prothonotary Warbler *(Protonotaria citrea)*, 76
Purple Gallinule *(Porphyrio martinica)*, 29
Purple Martin *(Progne subis)*, 59

R

Red-bellied Woodpecker *(Melanerpes carolinus)*, 50
Red-breasted Merganser *(Mergus serrator)*, 8
Red-breasted Nuthatch *(Sitta canadensis)*, 63
Red-cockaded Woodpecker *(Picoides borealis)*, 51
Red-eyed Vireo *(Vireo olivaceus)*, 58
Red-headed Woodpecker *(Melanerpes erythrocephalus)*, 50
Red Knot *(Calidris canutus)*, 35
Red-shouldered Hawk *(Buteo lineatus)*, 25
Red-tailed Hawk *(Buteo jamaicensis)*, 26

Red-throated Loon *(Gavia stellata)*, 10
Red-winged Blackbird *(Agelaius phoeniceus)*, 85
Ring-billed Gull *(Larus delewarensis)*, 39
Ring-necked Duck *(Aythya collaris)*, 5
Rock Pigeon (Columba livia), 43
Royal Tern *(Thalasseus maxima)*, 41
Ruby-crowned Kinglet *(Regulus calendula)*, 67
Ruby-throated Hummingbird *(Archilochus colubris)*, 49
Ruddy Duck *(Oxyura jamaicensis)*, 9
Ruddy Turnstone *(Arenaria interpres)*, 35
Rusty Blackbird *(Euphagus carolinus)*, 86

S

Sanderling *(Calidris alba)*, 36
Sandwich Tern *(Thalasseus sandvicensis)*, 42
Seaside Sparrow *(Ammodramus maritimus)*, 82
Semipalmated Plover *(Charadrius semipalmatus)*, 31
Snowy Egret *(Egretta thula)*, 17
Song Sparrow *(Melospiza melodia)*, 82
Sora *(Porzana carolina)*, 28
Spotted Sandpiper *(Actitus macularius)*, 33
Summer Tanager *(Piranga rubra)*, 83
Surf Scoter *(Melanitta perspicillata)*, 6

Swallow-tailed Kite *(Elanoides forficatus)*, 22

T

Tree Swallow *(Tachycineta bicolor)*, 60
Tricolored Heron *(Egretta tricolor)*, 18
Tufted Titmouse *(Baeolophus bicolor)*, 62
Turkey Vulture *(Cathartes aura)*, 21

W

Western Sandpiper *(Calidris mauri)*, 36
White-breasted Nuthatch *(Sitta carolinensis)*, 62
White-eyed Vireo *(Vireo griseus)*, 56
White Ibis *(Eudocimus albus)*, 20
White-throated Sparrow *(Zonotrichia albicollis)*, 83
Wild Turkey *(Meleagris gallopavo)*, 10

Willet *(Tringa semipalmatus)*, 34
Winter Wren *(Troglodytes hiemalis)*, 65
Wood Duck *(Aix sponsa)*, 2
Wood Stork *(Mycteria americana)*, 13
Wood Thrush *(Hylocichla mustelina)*, 69
Worm-eating Warbler *(Helmitheros vermivorum)*, 77

Y

Yellow-billed Cuckoo *(Coccyzus americanus)*, 45
Yellow-breasted Chat *(Icteria virens)*, 79
Yellow-crowned Night-Heron *(Nyctanassa violacea)*, 20
Yellow-rumped Warbler *(Dendroica coronata coronata)*, 73
Yellow-throated Vireo *(Vireo flavifrons)*, 57
Yellow-throated Warbler *(Dendroica dominica)*, 74

About the Author/Illustrator

Todd Telander is a naturalist, illustrator, and artist living in Walla Walla, Washington. He has studied and illustrated wildlife since 1988, while living in California, Colorado, New Mexico, and Washington. He graduated from the University of California at Santa Cruz with degrees in biology, environmental studies, and scientific illustration and has illustrated numerous books and other publications. His wife, Kirsten Telander, is a writer and teacher; they have two boys, Miles and Oliver. Todd's work can be viewed online at www.toddtelander.com.